More Praise for Anchored In

"When heartbreaking seasons shake us to our core, we often grab for everything other than God. But Micah tenderly reminds us page after page that Jesus is the only true Anchor who will hold us, steady us, and bring us through to the other side of every storm."
—**Lysa TerKeurst**, *New York Times* best-selling author and president of Proverbs 31 Ministries

"As a friend and guide, Micah Maddox will walk with you through life's hard times and show you how, through God's power, you can get to the other side with greater freedom, strength and victory."
—**Holley Gerth**, *Wall Street Journal* best-selling author of *You're Already Amazing*

"There are times when life hurts deeply. Through the grief, struggles and pain, we need reassurance that we are not alone. Micah Maddox's book *Anchored In*, renews our hope and reminds us that God's power can carry us through the stormy seas of life. Through scripture, stories, and personal applications, Micah lovingly offers hope, victory, and strength for everyone's journey."
—**Karol Ladd**, author of *Thrive, Don't Simply Survive* and *Power of a Positive Woman*

"Life is hard. Most of us have learned that truth firsthand, the hard way. Trials, broken dreams, and the unexpected storms of life can leave us stuck in the past or numb in the present. *Anchored In* is more than a pep talk or quick-fix formula—it is a way of life. It should be required reading by every believer, whether your storm is in the past, the present, or looming on the horizon. Regardless of the forecast, grab a copy and get anchored in!"
—**Vicki Courtney**, best-selling author of *5 Conversations You Must Have with Your Daughter*, *Move On*, and *Rest Assured*

"Micah speaks about deep issues, pains, and struggles because she has been there. In the pages of *Anchored In*, you will find the healing hope of God. It's brave, authentic, and powerful."
—**Courtney DeFeo**, author of *In This House, We Will Giggle*

"When I watch the news each morning and feel the swirl of circumstances around me, it's easy to feel powerless in this crazy world. Micah reminds

us that it's not our job to be powerful. It's our gift to be connected to a powerful God. Through the vulnerable telling of her personal story and the timeless truths she embeds, Micah holds out a lifeline to us that's *Anchored In* hope."
—**Amy Carroll,** author of *Breaking Up with Perfect* and Proverbs 31 Ministries speaker and writer

"With tenderness and understanding garnered through personal experience, Micah Maddox points us to the healing power available to those who are anchored in relationship with Jesus Christ. Some shredded places in my heart have been mended."
—**Cindi Wood,** speaker and author of *Anonymous: Discovering the Somebody You Are to God*

"One of the purposes of an anchor is to keep the ship from drifting or being dragged by the wind. A drifting ship could easily be damaged. A drifting Christian faces the same hazard. There are many events, pressures, and influences that can cause us to drift in the Christian life. Micah has skillfully uncovered these areas while pointing us back to God's anchoring presence. The lessons and real-life stories in this book provide direction on how to anchor our lives in the Lord. You will be enriched by this devotional."
—**Francie Taylor,** vice president, Keep the Heart, LLC

"Do you desire to discover God's power regardless of your circumstances? Want to experience a deeper relationship anchored in the power and presence of the Holy Spirit? If so, you'll love *Anchored In*. Micah Maddox brilliantly unpacks the power and presence of God (available for our daily living) and helps readers break free from paralyzing problems to embrace God's propelling power for abundant living."
—**Julie Gorman,** cofounder of Married for a Purpose and author of *Two Are Better Than One: God Has a Purpose for Your Marriage*

"Micah's warm and engaging style feels like a conversation with a dear friend. She encourages her readers to run to the Lord through every circumstance of life and to experience His power in every part of their story. She reminds us that we serve a God who transforms, a God who gives us His power to face every situation, a God who gives victory through our surrender to Him. He is good, and Micah's heartfelt words remind us of that truth."
—**Kristin Schmucker,** author and founder of The Daily Grace Co.

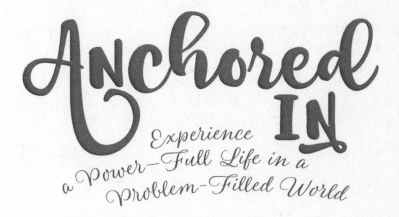

Anchored IN

Experience a Power-Full Life in a Problem-Filled World

MICAH MADDOX

ABINGDON PRESS
NASHVILLE

Library of Congress Cataloging-in-Publication Data has been requested.

ISBN 978-1-5018-4867-4

17 18 19 20 21 22 23 24 25—10 9 8 7 6 5 4 3 2 1
MANUFACTURED IN THE UNITED STATES OF AMERICA

*For my crew
because I love ya.*

Contents

Part 1: Past Power

Chapter 1: Power in the Deep 3

Chapter 2: Power in the Difficult 21

Chapter 3: Power in the Dark 40

Chapter 4: Power in the Dream 60

Part 2: Present Power

Chapter 5: Power in My Mind 79

Chapter 6: Power in My Heart 102

Chapter 7: Power in My Life 118

Contents

Part 3: Potential Power

Chapter 8: Power in Position 137

Chapter 9: Power in Perspective 156

Part 4: Anchored in the Promise of God's Presence

Chapter 10: Step 1: Listen to His Voice 173

Chapter 11: Step 2: Let God Define the Dream 196

Chapter 12: Step 3: Live in Victory 212

Acknowledgments 229

Notes 232

Part 1

Past Power

Chapter 1

Power in the Deep

*These things God has revealed to us
through the Spirit. For the Spirit searches
everything, even the depths of God.*
             —1 Corinthians 2:10

Where Is God?

After a long day of school, I reached for the lamp to turn out the light. Pulling the covers up to my chin, I let one tear seep out of my right eye, and I questioned God: "Why did my daddy leave me?" "Why doesn't my daddy love me?"

As the years went by, and after I had my own little girl, I looked deeply into her innocent eyes and asked God again, "How could a parent abandon his or her child?" I knew God had to have a purpose for my broken childhood, and I began a process of pressing harder and harder into places I could not understand, seeking a purpose in the problems that I endured as a result of my dad abandoning me. It was one of the deepest, hardest places of my life, yet God never left me. I experienced God's power as He carried me through the different stages of my desperation for a relationship with my biological father. The answer to why my dad left never came as I thought it would, but God's power propelled me through a healing process that cannot be explained by human words. It's one of the reasons I feel compelled to share God's power and presence with others because of its life-transforming ability.

Maybe in your life now or in the past you have wanted to see God's power preside over any type of problems you felt were unavoidable. Your journey may not include abandonment, but you know the unique sting of your own life's struggle. I imagine you picked up this book because you've experienced a problem or two in your life. Perhaps you've even presented your own questions before God. You aren't alone. We may never fully understand why we encounter such difficult things in our world, but we can begin to understand God's power as He binds up our wounds one by one and helps us understand the only way to live is anchored in His power.

Our world is filled with problems of corruption, dishonesty, upside-down finances, betrayal, and plenty of other factors. If you were to look at it simply with your own eyes, you may wonder, *Where is God's power when I need it most?*

There are moments in life that are so devastating there are no words to utter. You see people's lips moving, but you can't absorb the words due to the burden that consumes your mind. You try to move forward with a normal routine, but the world seems to move in slow motion as problems persist, paralyzing your best efforts to press on. Life can hurt deeply. It can scar the tender parts of your heart and make you feel like your life is completely drenched in a sea of problems that cannot be remedied.

The truth is, there is a remedy. There is someone who anchors us, and He holds all power to overcome every problem we face. But accessing His power sometimes seems impossible. Living anchored, grounded, and full of His power feels out of reach. Life is manageable when bills are paid, kids are healthy, marriage is working, church is delightful, and work is enjoyable. When test results reveal a serious illness or when a marriage is sitting on the edge of disaster, the stability of life lingers with unknown possibilities, and we quickly forget the anchor that once held us securely. Unexpected bills, heartbreaking conversations, and a life of heavy burdens unload themselves into a world that seems to be shattering right before our eyes. I know this to be true because just like you, I have a list of desperate moments when I needed much more than the world offers.

No one ever plans it this way, but there are people all around us holding shattered pieces of life, wanting desperately to put the pieces together again. We convince ourselves that if our problems would go away, we could get on with our lives and live a powerful life of fulfillment. But problems continue, and we can't seem to get out of the cycle of each current pulling us deeper and deeper into the problems we would rather avoid. Sometimes it feels as if the anchor of our soul has been ripped from the deepest depth of our hearts, and our ship of life is lost at sea. The waters rise, and the trials, troubles, and struggles take center stage, filling us with a void of power.

What is a desperate, hurting soul to do when life is filled

to the brim with problems? Cling to the power and presence of God. If you know Him, He's already with you. Right there, in the midst of the unpredictable, He knows every single detail of your life. He is an anchor that does not budge. When everything in life is in disarray, God's presence is constant, firm, secure.

> But you shall cling to the Lord your God, just as you have done to this day. (Joshua 23:8)

Our deepest moments of life are often the ones that draw us into the presence of God more authentically than ever before, or they push us so far away that we cannot see, hear, or remember what it feels like to be close to Him. When it seems like God is far away and the winds of life continue to billow overhead, it's normal to try to achieve nearness to God by doing more for Him or by striving to ignite the inner strength we know we hold. The problem is that power is not something we can muster up when we think we need a fresh dose of the Holy Spirit. It goes much deeper than a prayer of crisis at the moment of an emergency. We must know that God's power is present every moment of our life.

The biggest problem we face is not a lack of God's power; it's realizing where real power comes from.

The Holy Spirit does not blow in like the north wind on a fall day, shaking every leaf of our lives to the ground as we wonder whether we will be able to withstand the storm. He indwells every believer at the moment we choose to accept Jesus Christ into our lives and consistently remains present and accessible no matter what our lives look or feel like. When the wind of life rushes in and we are shaken, we have what it takes within our own bodies to stand firm and be grounded, anchored, and tethered to the greatest power ever known. The biggest problem we face is not a lack of God's power; it's realizing where real power comes from. It doesn't come from you, and it doesn't come from me. It comes from the Holy Spirit of God within each and every believer.

> If the Spirit of him who raised Jesus from the dead dwells in you, he who raised Christ Jesus from the dead will also give life to your mortal bodies through his Spirit who dwells in you. (Romans 8:11)

Until we fully and completely accept that real power comes from God and God alone, we will never really experience it. The power that we desperately desire is distinctly divine. Sometimes we get glimpses of it from a book, a sermon, or a song, but if we want to experience it every day, there is only one way.

God's power is present in people who pursue it.

The Deepest Places

It seems it's in the deepest places of life, when there is nowhere else to turn, that our hearts sincerely press completely and fully into the power of the Holy Spirit. Pursuing God becomes a thing that we do when we have nowhere else to turn. That's when I have experienced God for myself. It's in those moments that forced me to my knees that I cried out with all my heart and soul for God to show up. Those deep, unpredictable places where I know the Holy Spirit spoke to my heart—I don't ever want to trade those. It's not that I enjoy the problems that filled my life to overflowing, but I know in the difficult moments when I knelt before God, He was with me. Why does it take so much for us to fall to our knees? God's power is worthy of worship before worry sets in.

Let's begin this beautiful journey of experiencing God's power by looking back over the problems of our lives and re-membering the times God's power has sustained us in the past. When we rediscover the moments God's power was with us in the past, we will be ready to face the problems of the future.

When I look back over the deep waters of my life, I tend to raise the question, why? Isn't that what we all think when a devastating tragedy hits, or when life doesn't look the way we think it should? Why would God, who loves me, allow this? I know some people would say we should never question God, but I've learned it's in my questions that I get answers. The answers don't always look like the explanation I want, but God's answers are better than that. God's answers are filled with power.

Some of my precious friends have walked through some of the deepest places I've ever heard of, yet they continue to press forward in God's power, refusing to let the problems of this world take them under. It's not because they are amazing women, strong beyond measure, but because they've learned to press into the power of God amid the deep places of life. And for that they are amazing. They have experienced the power of God's presence in moments when they had no more prayers, no more tears, and no more words.

As you read their breathtaking moments, consider how they've survived. It's only by the power of the Holy Spirit of God. When we remember the power we are anchored to, even in the deep places of our past, we will begin to experience God for who He really is—the anchor of everything we are. You and I hold the unique ability to access the power of God in the deep just like these women.

Brenda

The memory of the phone call still knocks the wind out of her. Her adult son's car was found on a bridge from which he jumped to his own death. The result was complete devastation. He left five children with no daddy and their precious mother, who was fighting to make a life for them. And then there's *his* mother, Brenda, struggling with her own health issues, wondering why God would allow such tragedy to be a part of their story. Grief is tragic, but Brenda and the entire family would tell you, "Jesus carried us every step of the way."

Sharon

A little girl is now all grown up and blessed with grandchildren. The memories of her childhood still come to mind, and the desire to help others avoid such abuse compels her to speak up about protecting girls, even in their own homes. Trusting men is difficult for her. For years this part of her story has gone around and around in her mind. As a grandmother, she is finally able to break the silence and fill it with truth through God's power.

Bryn

Her son, Carson, is ill. The doctors have no answers. He's young and housebound with no strength. Where is God? Although discouragement creeps in at every turn, Carson and Bryn boldly give God glory in spite of the long hospital stays and lack of answers. God's presence is obvious in their lives even though He has not fixed their problem. But He offers them His power in the midst of their struggle, and that is what they need most.

Sara

She watched her big sister suffer a long, hard battle through cancer that ultimately took her teenage life much too soon. Sara deals with the decision to be angry with God or seek peace and comfort in His presence. The concerns about her own health and the health of her daughter cause questions and concern. She's a pastor's wife who has given her entire life to lead others to the only power that has sustained her through the ups and downs.

Tamara (My Mama)

Her husband of twelve years, a pastor, left her and her children, never to return. How does a woman suddenly fill the role of both mom and dad? Loving again, trusting again, and starting over seemed impossible. Her story is amazing. After a while, she remarried. Clay was a godly man who raised her children to serve God no matter what. Both of her adult children are serving in church ministry. Tamara would tell you, "God didn't bring us this far to leave us." By His power, her children share the message of God's presence through the deep waters of life.

Wendy

After months of waiting for her precious bundle of joy, her baby was stillborn; she was left with an empty crib with no coos or cuddles—only silence. The joy she'd anticipated was crushed, destroyed, and taken from her hands before she could enjoy the gift of a child. Why would God allow such tragedy? Wendy has written a book about her losses to encourage those who walk the same path. Through God's power Wendy's story is bringing people hope in one of the deepest, darkest places of life.

The first key to experiencing God's power is knowing the power we desire comes only from Him.

Judith

She's a strong woman. A breast cancer survivor fighting for a long life, and no more cancer to invade her body and steal the good cells. The regular tests cause anxiety, and waiting for the results is agonizing. Her source of strength does not come in a physical form but a heavenly one. She knows God and His presence carries her day and night.

Ashley

She and her husband have tried for years to conceive, but the result is always the same: negative. Feeling as though God has forgotten her consumes her heart and mind as she watches her sisters and friends fill up their homes with the joy of children. Ashley has learned to find peace in God's presence regardless of her heart's desire to be a mother.

It's easy to look at others and see what they need. We can look over a friend's shoulder and know he or she needs comfort, grace, time, or a counselor. When it's our own problem, though, it's much harder to define, especially when we feel like we aren't getting what we need from God. When we feel unsatisfied with God and His power, we begin to look around for other sources of strength, hope, and love. Often we will exercise our own willpower or determination to fill the void of what is missing, but then we come up empty every time. God's power is the only source of strength that will sustain us.

The first key to experiencing God's power is knowing the power we desire comes only from Him.

The Choice

When we look back over our lives and remember the deep issues, problems, events, and pains, we have a choice to make. We can decide to discover God at new depths, or we can become discouraged all over again. There have been times in my own life when I have allowed myself to become extremely discouraged when I recall things that have occurred in my life. When my dad abandoned me, I didn't realize how it would affect my life long-term. It's frustrating when something that happened so long ago still feels fresh. So I am faced with a choice every single day. I can press into the depth of the abandonment, I can run from it, or I can call on God.

In Jonah 2, Jonah finds himself in the deepest place of all: the belly of a fish in the deep blue sea. Although Jonah made a mistake that landed him there, his attitude is the same as mine when I recall deep places. As soon as I realize I'm without escape and at the end of my rope, that's when I cry out to the Lord just like Jonah.

> When my life was fainting away, I remembered the LORD,
> and my prayer came to you, into your holy temple.
>
> (Jonah 2:7)

What if you and I remembered the Lord every time we face deep places in our lives? If we could learn to press into the power that we know is available rather than rehashing our problems again and again—or worse, running from them—we would be able to experience God's presence in transformative ways in areas of our lives that we have given up on ever changing. God is our anchor in the deepest, roughest waters.

The power of God is not about avoiding the deep waters of life. It's about diving into them. Diving into my problems or rehashing the old ones is not something that I love to do. It's hard. But here's the thing I have learned: the longer I try to press down my problems, and the longer I try to leave my problems behind, the stronger they bind me. The power I want to have over what has happened to me is what actually over-powers me. It consumes my thoughts and causes my life to feel consumed with the depth of my situation.

But in facing reality I am able to accept the facts of my life. One fact for me is that I was left to find life with God without the love of my biological father. Your facts will look different. Maybe you were abused, unloved, lonely, or rejected, or per-haps your relationships never work out quite right. Or maybe you haven't lost a parent, but a disease has stolen his or her mind, and the effects on your emotions cause grief too heavy to bear. That's your deep place. We all have at least one deep place. When we think of our lives, our deep place often seems to be what we define ourselves by rather than who God is in our lives.

Paul had a deep place too. In 2 Corinthians 12:8-10 (AMP), we see how it affected him. Examine the result of pressing into the deep place of Paul's life:

> Concerning this I pleaded with the Lord three times that it might leave me; but He has said to me, "My grace is sufficient for you [My lovingkindness and My mercy are more than enough—always available—regardless of the situation]; for [My] power is being perfected [and is completed and shows itself most effectively] in [your] weakness." Therefore, I will all the more gladly boast in my weaknesses, so that the power of Christ [may completely enfold me and] may dwell in me. So I am well pleased

with weaknesses, with insults, with distresses, with
persecutions, and with difficulties, for the sake of Christ;
for when I am weak [in human strength], then I am strong
[truly able, truly powerful, truly drawing from God's
strength].

Even through the biggest distress and difficult situations
of life, Paul knew that divine power didn't come from human
strength. The beauty in this is that it applies to us too. No matter how weak we feel because of what we have been through or
are going through, we have access to divine power through the
Holy Spirit of God. Divine power delivers people.

I promise if you will stick with me through the end of this
book, your deep place will be transformed from your greatest problem to the greatest power you have ever experienced.
Your problem-filled world will be filled with power before you
know it. God does that. He transforms lives. He's transformed
mine, and He has the power to transform yours as you anchor
yourself in His presence.

In the next chapter I will share the details of my story, and
my prayer is that by opening up my vulnerable places in life,
you will see God's power, feel God's presence, and know that
you can face the very thing you have tried to forget. Our past
is powerful in regard to our future, yet God has a purpose for
the deep places we have trodden. It's time to dive into these
places of unrest in order to put them to rest. Are you ready?
Take a deep breath, and let's travel these deep waters together.
God's power resides there, and although the journey might be

difficult, the Holy Spirit's presence is more powerful than any of our problems.

At the end of each chapter you will find a few questions, a prayer, and a passage to encourage you as you ponder your own experience with God and His power. Take time to allow God to speak to your heart. As you pray, listen to what God is saying to you. If you hear a specific message from the Holy Spirit, record it in the space provided. When you write down what God is doing in your life as you look below the surface at the deep places in your heart, you will have a beautiful record to help you recall God's presence and the way His power has worked in your life in the past.

Questions to Ponder

1. What is a deep place in your life?

2. How have you experienced God's power in the past?

3. How have you seen God's power obviously working in someone else's life?

4. In what ways does that challenge or encourage you?

5. In what area of your life do you need God most right now?

Praying God's Power

Dear Heavenly Father,

You know the moments in my life that have taken me to the depths of the sea. You know my questions, my fears, and my failures. As I look back over my life and remember the difficult landmarks, I want to see You. I want to know that You have a purpose in it all. As I take this journey of experiencing your power as never before, show me how to press deeper into Your power regardless of what I've been through. I need You to be my anchor.

In Jesus' name, amen.

Experiencing God's Presence

Deep calls to deep
   at the roar of your waterfalls;
all your breakers and your waves
   have gone over me.
By day the LORD commands his steadfast love,
   and at night his song is with me,
   a prayer to the God of my life.
I say to God, my rock:
   "Why have you forgotten me?
Why do I go mourning
   because of the oppression of the enemy?"
As with a deadly wound in my bones,
   my adversaries taunt me,
while they say to me all the day long,
   "Where is your God?"

Why are you cast down, O my soul,
   and why are you in turmoil within me?
Hope in God; for I shall again praise him,
   my salvation and my God.

—Psalm 42:7-11

Chapter 2

Power in the Difficult

Give ear to my words, O Lord;
consider my groaning.
Give attention to the sound of my cry,
my King and my God,
for to you do I pray.
—Psalm 5:1-2

Once Upon a Time...

*T*here is a desire inside every little girl to be loved, cherished, and adored by her daddy. Just the word *daddy* makes me want to cuddle up with a warm blanket and listen to a deep voice tell a story of a princess being captivated by a winsome prince on a white horse. When the story is done and no more words are spoken, daddy swoops up his little girl, and they twirl through the kitchen to the sound of their favorite song. Every good daddy-daughter duo has a song—at least that's the way I imagine it.

My story doesn't take place in the kitchen. There's no dancing, and I don't remember cuddles with my main man. Although

I longed for a dad who would love me and be proud of me, I never really knew my biological dad. My memories consist of him going to the church early to prepare the sermon. He would study long hours and return home long after I was in bed. I don't have memories of sitting in his lap, but I do remember watching him. He would hold the Bible the same way every Sunday. When the music began for the invitation, he would bow his head, rest his elbow on his other arm, and pinch the top of his nose as people flooded the altar. I knew my daddy was the best preacher ever. He would proclaim the Word of God, and even my little five-year-old mind and heart would be pierced with conviction. He was the closest thing to God that I knew.

Maybe you have someone in your life whom you once idolized, looked up to, or admired. Perhaps that person slowly gained your trust or his or her position held prominence and required respect, like my dad's did. Being the pastor's daughter, I looked up to the preacher. My earliest memories are of hymnals, suits, and kisses on the cheek from old women who wore perfume that would stick to my clothes the entire day.

We entered the church and sat down in the same pew where we always sat. We sang a few songs, and Daddy approached the pulpit to preach. As he finished his sermon and the music began, I tugged on my mama's dress. "I want to ask Jesus into my heart," I said. I could barely get the words out without crying. My emotions still run raw just as they did that day. I've always been a crier. I knew I was a sinner, and I needed Jesus to forgive me and save me. I knew I couldn't make it to heaven on my own. I wanted to follow Jesus and live for Him. My mom and I knelt down on the front pew, and I prayed, asking Jesus to forgive me of my sins and come into my heart and life and save me from an eternal hell. I remember imagining Jesus knocking softly on the door of my heart as I opened it. He came in and held me close. My relationship with Jesus began.

Days and months passed, and it was the same routine. Mama took care of me and my brother, and Daddy worked long hours at the church. One Sunday morning, after Dad headed to church, the rest of us loaded into the old gray Oldsmobile. We pulled into the church parking lot and noticed Daddy's car was not in the normal spot. As we surveyed the parking lot, we realized his car wasn't there at all. Mama swiftly headed toward the church office, my brother and I following closely behind. We opened the big wooden door, and I skipped over to the couch, where my ruffles fell softly on the leather cushions. I looked up and saw Mama reading a note that had been left behind. My dad was gone and he wasn't coming back. Mama fell to her knees, hugged us close, and began to cry out to God. Not really understanding what was going on and what the note meant, I began to cry too. Why did Daddy leave? Where did he go? Who would preach the Sunday morning message? Why were Mama and my brother so sad? He is coming back, isn't he? It was too much for my little mind to comprehend.

I watched as Mama put her shoulders back and dried her tears. She found the head deacon and told him he would need to preach the morning service. That was the Sunday morning that Daddy abandoned the church, Mama, my brother, and me. There would be no fairy tales and cuddles or deep voice telling a bedtime story. Daddy was gone, and he wasn't coming back.

I'm sure you've heard other stories much like mine where a man of God makes a big mistake. Or maybe for you it was a mother who walked out of her children's lives, not realizing the irreversible impact on those little lives. Perhaps a leader of a big corporation was caught stealing money or the nice man down the street was convicted of sexually assaulting children. Difficult stuff is everywhere. It affects each of us in one way or another. Living anchored in God's power doesn't take the difficult stuff away, but it does allow us to walk through the difficult days without drowning. When I think back on that day and the way my mom put her shoulders back and lifted her head, I now understand where her determination, resolve, and confidence came from. She had the power of God within her. It wasn't her own determination or resolve to survive and thrive beyond the choices of another; it was God's unimaginable strength that lifted her chin and calmed her shattered heart.

God's Power Revealed

I remember the vivid feelings when I was nine of not being wanted by my dad—my pastor and my hero. He signed off all rights to me and disowned me. It was official and final. I was no longer his daughter, and he was no longer my father. I was disowned, abandoned, and unloved by the man who was supposed to protect, love, and one day give me away to my Prince Charming. How does a girl recover from a loss that difficult?

God had a plan in spite of my dad's sinful mistakes. A

guardian angel named Clay Potter swooped up our broken family and taught us how to love and be loved. He came into our lives and loved us like we were his own. He taught me loyalty to God and His Word. He wasn't a fairy-tale type of guy. Clay didn't like warm cuddles and dancing, but he gave me much more than that: an example of what it means to love God with all of your heart. He taught me how a man should love his wife. He wasn't a pastor; he didn't even talk much. He was quiet, meek, and loving. That describes him perfectly.

In my teen years, Clay became my biggest encourager. He told me I could succeed. When I felt insecure, he affirmed me. He taught me to love the unlovable. Our weekends weren't spent putting on a show at church but rather going to the local mission and singing "Wonderful Words of Life" and "Love Lifted Me" to people who were at rock bottom. Clay had a past of pain and heartache. As an alcoholic, he met Jesus after a bad accident that almost took the life of his best friend. He showed me how to reach the unreachable for Jesus because he knew personally what it felt like to be unreachable. He was much better than a fairy-tale daddy who danced in the kitchen. Clay gave me hope in spite of my broken heart. He helped me find my anchor again.

My sweet mama, always faithful and kind, continually pointed us to Jesus by quoting verses like, "What time I am afraid, I will trust in thee" (Psalm 56:3 KJV) and "Trust in the Lord with all thine heart; and lean not unto thine own understanding. In all thy ways, acknowledge him, and he shall direct thy paths" (Proverbs 3:5-6 KJV). She would say, "God didn't bring us this far to leave us." Her faithful example of turning to God in difficult circumstances taught us to turn to Him also. Mama was a steadfast example of a woman anchored in the power of God.

As a teenager, I resolved that I would see my biological dad on the other side of this life. I imagined walking up to him in heaven, a place without any more pain or heartache. I wouldn't feel the ache in my soul of being unloved and left behind. I wouldn't look into his eyes and be angry. I would feel loved, secure, and calm. I said good night to my pain and tucked it away in the farthest space of my heart.

I don't know what pain you've experienced in your life, but I do know we all have a past. When we tuck it away and pretend it never happened, we waste something that God can use. Pretending our problems don't exist does not do away with them; it only compounds them. What if God can take that broken childhood, that difficult event, that shattered piece of your heart and help someone? I know it's hard to look at trials through a lens of "helping others," but it's become a way of life for me. When I get my eyes off of what happened to me and onto what God has done for me, I am able to share my story with a slice of hope rather than horror.

My past helps me pursue God more. When I remember all God has done, I know He is able to help me, hold me, and anchor me in my hard times.

Unanswered Questions

It had been twenty-three years since I had heard his voice. I had not seen his face. I had no contact with him. As an adult

I would look into the eyes of men his age and wonder why he left me. The issues I had put to bed were beginning to awaken. I had cried myself to sleep a lot as a little girl but pressed the pain as far away as possible through my teenage years. As a grown woman, I began to revisit the same old questions that appeared in my heart, mind, and soul. I found myself on my tear-soaked pillow, trying not to make a sound. I felt like a little girl in a woman's body struggling for acceptance from my dad. My body thrashed, and I sobbed uncontrollably. I was heart-broken that my daddy would leave me all those years ago. Did he not love me? How could he not? I could not understand as a little girl, but now the grief was uncontainable. I had my own children who were close to my age when he had left. I would look into their eyes and wonder what he must have thought when he looked at me for the last time. I could not comprehend what would compel him to abandon me.

It was a fall day. As the leaves fluttered through the air, thoughts of my dad fluttered through my mind. I wanted to find him and look into his eyes. I searched the Internet for his picture, and when I found one, I stared. I looked deep into his eyes and tried to make sense of it all…and I cried.

The Search

I was home alone. The house was quiet. The kids were at school, and I had exactly two hours before their arrival. As I'd done many days before, I sat at the computer and searched for him. Maybe there would be another picture that would give me more answers. Maybe today I could see and understand. Maybe I could find an address and send a letter expressing my deepest thoughts. I could let him know how much I had missed having him in my life. I could send him a picture of my husband and children. I could tell him how I earned the Most Valuable Player award in volleyball my senior year. I could sing him a song with my husband and let him be proud of what I had become. Fairy-tale dreams still flooded my adult mind.

Forgiveness

I continued my search, and then I found it: a phone number connected to a name and an address that had to be his. With trembling hands, I sent this text: "It's Micah. How is my dad?" Immediately I got a response: "Can he call you?" I was shocked, and before I knew what I was doing, I typed "Yes." It struck me that I should think about this, but it was too late—the phone was ringing. It rang once, twice, and on the third ring I knew if I did not pick up, I might never feel compelled to talk again. I picked up the call ready to offer

> Whatever the difficult thing is in your life that keeps you awake at night, threatening the anchor of your soul, God is bigger and wiser.

the forgiveness that I needed to release. Immediately I heard his voice, and in my mind I became five years old again as we both sobbed. He said, "I'm sorry." I quickly replied, "I forgive you." I could see him resting his elbow on his opposite arm, pinching his nose right at the top. We talked for a few minutes, and he said he would like to talk again. I agreed. I hung up the phone, and for the first time in years, a heavy weight was lifted. I was finally free from the pain of abandonment. I did it! I said, "I forgive you," and I did truly forgive.

> "Our Father in heaven,
> hallowed be your name.
> Your kingdom come,
> your will be done,
>   on earth as it is in heaven.
> Give us this day our daily bread,
> and forgive us our debts,
>   as we also have forgiven our debtors.
> And lead us not into temptation,
>   but deliver us from evil.

For if you forgive others their trespasses, your heavenly Father will also forgive you, but if you do not forgive others their trespasses, neither will your Father forgive your trespasses." (Matthew 6:9-15)

Freedom

When my husband got home, I told him what I had done. He was shocked. He held me and told me he was proud of me. I woke up the next several days proud and excited for what my new life with my dad would look like. I imagined phone calls just to say I love you. Maybe notes in the mail would begin to appear. My big dream was that he would walk into my church while I was up on the stage, singing, and we would run into each other's arms and begin our new life as daddy and daughter.

Bondage

The next call was about three weeks later. This call was a little less exciting and freeing; in fact it was devastating. He never said what I imagined he would say. It wasn't the fairy-tale, happy-movie ending every girl dreams of. There were words that hurt, pierced, and kept me up at night all over again. Words of justifying his actions and using the Bible as his backing shot through the phone like arrows from the enemy. Lies, worldly reasoning, and selfish motives were spoken until I could not listen to another word. I quickly replied, "I have to go." I hung up the phone in a mess of tears. My heart, which had been so lifted and free, was now bound in the tightest bondage I had ever experienced. I found myself back on my pillow, bawling my eyes out with no way to navigate through the feelings and the hurt. Then the questions began in my head. *Why did I allow him to call in the first place? What was I thinking?* I knew better. I knew it wouldn't be what I expected. I should have never contacted him, and I welcomed sleepless nights back into my life.

I went through a very difficult time trying to figure out how to deal with all of the enormous feelings. They consumed me for months. It was like being abandoned all over again. As if the first time wasn't bad enough, now I was old enough to truly understand what was going on, and it was heart-wrenching. It affected my relationship with my husband because I could not verbalize what was going on in my mind and heart. It was too painful to talk about. And what good would it do to talk about it? No one could understand or fix it. I'm sure you have your own thing that needs fixing. Wouldn't it be lovely if we could just fix each other's problems? You fix mine, I'll fix yours, and we will all live happily ever after. If only.

Whatever the difficult thing is in your life that keeps you awake at night, threatening the anchor of your soul, God is bigger and wiser. Living anchored and trusting God with every situation in life isn't something that just happens overnight. It's a commitment to live surrendered to the Savior no matter how difficult the situation in life becomes. During this season I learned more about God as my anchor than I ever had before. Although it wasn't easy, I did learn what it meant to live in the peace of God that passes all understanding. When your soul is consumed with heartache, there's no way to overcome it without God's power and presence. His Word became my place of retreat and restoration when I felt bruised and betrayed. Living anchored in God's power is the fix I've found for my deepest wounds. His power sustains me when I can't press on and lifts me when I feel like sinking.

Freedom

I was not magically healed from every pain I ever felt. The Holy Spirit of God came into my living room day after day and gave me a verse, a word, a comforting embrace. Memories did not get blotted out with a permanent marker never to resurface again, but God's power filled my heart day by day as God reminded me through His Word that He is my heavenly Father, who will never leave me or forsake me. The broken places that once ached with the need to be accepted and loved were filled with my heavenly Father's mercy, love, truth, and power.

Am I over it? There are some things in life you never forget, but you must forgive. There is power in forgiveness. Power to stay bound or power to let the anchor of God hold you close as you choose to let go of the one thing that has held on to you for years—the most difficult thing. Power comes when we know God is bigger than our pain, and forgiveness is more freeing than the failure of someone we love. I had a season when my pain consumed every part of me. I had to choose to not allow the unanswered questions to reign in my mind anymore. God guided me to His perfect love and away from the idea that a daddy's love should be perfect. Through the power of the Holy Spirit, I found peace beyond my pain and hope beyond my hurt. I learned to live anchored in my heavenly Father's actions rather than my earthly father's. Power in the difficult is found when we make the choice to forgive, love, and live anchored to Jesus and no one else.

I still cry sometimes. But I don't sob myself to sleep hopeless, lonely, or feeling betrayed. I cry because God has been faithful. He set me free from heavy chains placed around me as a little girl. They were much too heavy to carry alone. Only Jesus could cut them loose and carry them away. It has taken time and many tears, prayers, and nights of asking why, but God has soothed the ache deep in my heart, which once yearned for answers.

God's power overwhelms my soul. It's not because I'm a special girl who loves God and never faces my feelings. It's because God helped me in my weakness to face my biggest fear of all. When I heard my dad's voice, God's peace said, "You did the right thing." I don't need fairy tales and white horses or a deep voice telling a princess story. My Father is the King of kings and Lord of lords. His stories of golden streets, sparkling crowns, and a place of no more pain speak words of hope and power louder and deeper than any human voice. I love cuddling up close to Him. His warm embrace is more real than anything I've ever experienced. He is my anchor.

Although my daddy hurt me deeply, I love my dad. He is a big part of who I have become. No legal document can change DNA. I don't agree with my dad's choices, but God set me free from the bondage of a hopeless identity. I have three fathers now: a biological one, who taught me how to forgive when it seemed impossible; an earthly one, who taught me how to be faithful and loving; and a heavenly one, whom words cannot describe. My heavenly Father fills the voids and heals the wounds when I try to tuck them away in the deepest places of my heart. He anchors me. As we continue walking through the pages of this book together, I pray you will find the key to

> *Peace in the Father's arms is the most precious thing on earth.*

living anchored in God's power beyond the problems of this life—it's a beautiful place to live.

If issues in your life continually resurface and cause you to relive and rehash past pain, let me throw you a life raft. Peace in the Father's arms is the most precious thing on earth. If you struggle to find assurance, seek Him with all your heart. If the pain you feel can't be put into words, Jesus understands. He knows the deepest ache inside. He sees when you're alone. If your life is less than a fairy tale, it's time to let Jesus swoop you up, carry you to the kitchen, and dance to your daddy-daughter song. If you don't have one, let me share one of mine with you:

Overwhelmed

By Micah Maddox

So overwhelmed by your goodness,
So overwhelmed by your grace,
In awe of your forgiveness,
And your mercy in this place.
You are good to me,
You are grace so free,
You are peace,
You are rest to my weary soul.

Difficult circumstances often carry us to the deepest water we've ever experienced. Rough waters are too much for us to handle alone. God knows. It's time to hold on to His strength, His will, His way, His Word. It's time to live anchored in His power.

Questions to Ponder

1. What pain have you tried to put to bed, never to deal with again?

2. How has it affected your life?

3. What do you think the outcome would be if you truly handed over your hardest circumstances to God's control?

4. Who in your life do you need to forgive? Journal your thoughts of how you might be able to take steps to forgive that person.

Praying God's Power

Dear Heavenly Father,

I need You. When life seems too heavy and too complicated, I know You see the big picture. Help me rest in Your love and care when memories flood my mind. Help me see You clearly in the struggles, and carry me when I can't carry on. Give me hope to move forward and grace to get through the hardest days. Please guide me to the place of peace, where I can rest secure and calm. I need to hear Your voice. I need to feel Your embrace. I want to cuddle up in Your lap. I want to stay with You awhile. Thank You for loving me.

In Jesus' name, amen.

Experiencing God's Presence

Give ear to my words, O Lord;
    consider my groaning.
Give attention to the sound of my cry,
    my King and my God,
       for to you do I pray.
O Lord, in the morning you hear my voice;
    in the morning I prepare a sacrifice for you
       and watch.

For you are not a God who delights in
       wickedness;
    evil may not dwell with you.
The boastful shall not stand before your eyes;
    you hate all evildoers.
You destroy those who speak lies;
    the Lord abhors the bloodthirsty and
       deceitful man.

But I, through the abundance of your steadfast
       love,
    will enter your house.
I will bow down toward your holy temple
    in the fear of you.
Lead me, O Lord, in your righteousness
    because of my enemies;
       make your way straight before me.

For there is no truth in their mouth;
   their inmost self is destruction;
their throat is an open grave;
   they flatter with their tongue.
Make them bear their guilt, O God;
   let them fall by their own counsels;
because of the abundance of their transgressions
     cast them out,
   for they have rebelled against you.

But let all who take refuge in you rejoice;
   let them ever sing for joy,
and spread your protection over them,
   that those who love your name may exult
     in you.
For you bless the righteous, O Lord;
   you cover him with favor as with a shield.

—Psalm 5

Chapter 3

Power in the Dark

Yea, though I walk through the valley of
the shadow of death, I will fear no evil:
for thou art with me; thy rod and thy
staff they comfort me.
—*Psalm 23:4 (KJV)*

In Sickness and in Health

We were all of sixteen when our eyes met for the first time at high school orientation. He was taller than all of my friends, and his blue eyes captured my gaze so much that I followed him all over the high school as we met our teachers and learned about our class schedule for our eleventh-grade year. I found out later that he thought I was pretty cute too. Eeeek! I say that in my best teenage-girl squeal with my hands fanning my face. Fast-forward through a few high school crushes and some breakups that we won't dwell on, and we were destined for marriage. No, really. In January of that school year he asked me to be his girlfriend, and the rest is history—sort of. Rob wanted to be in the ministry, and

40

little did he know that at the age of fourteen, I had told God I would marry a pastor if that's what He had for me. This was confirmation that Rob was the man for me, and we were the perfect match!

We married five years later and began the journey of our lives. The babies started coming. The first was a girl. The second was a girl. And with prayers and tears, the third was a boy. And we were done. At least that's the way we planned it, but more about that later. After a few moves and several years in ministry, I found myself in an emergency room with the love of my life. I sat in the hard plastic

> Darkness is only a distraction. It does not mean God has departed.

chair as he lay on the gurney, writhing in pain. We waited for test results, but one by one the results came back normal.

In the coming weeks I watched as my healthy young husband deteriorated right before my eyes. It began with sleeping a lot and then not wanting to eat. His big, hearty frame began to shrink, and his smile that usually lit up a room began to fade. His countenance was strained, full of pain and turmoil. I was afraid and worried. Rob was falling apart physically, and I was falling apart emotionally.

We prayed for God to take the pain away, to heal the unknown. But God was silent. This was the beginning of a season of darkness when we learned a lot about the power of the presence of God in the dark seasons of life. In *Objects of His Affection*, Scotty Smith shares these powerful words: "Interestingly enough, the most-asked question in the whole Bible—from Genesis to Revelation—is 'How long, O Lord, how long?' And the most repeated command from God is 'Do not fear' or 'Do not be afraid.' The people of God consistently cry out for relief, and the God of love bids us trust him."[1] That's exactly where I was—needing to trust and rely on God. God was calling me to rely on Him, but the lack of answers sounded like silence rather than a call of comfort to my worried ears.

Waiting

Kneeling on my kitchen floor, surrounded by dropped Cheerios from yesterday's breakfast seemed to be how I always landed—knees pressed to the cold tile floor, hands gripping my Bible, tears dripping from my trembling chin as I asked God *why* for the four hundredth time. I had heard that His line was never busy and that He cared for me, but in this moment it seemed as though He had forgotten me. Trying to recall the verses about God never leaving, I wanted to remember that He hears me when I call, but no answers were coming. I must not be doing it right. Maybe I should lay prostrate, not eat for days, or perhaps lock myself in my closet and wait for Him to show up in physical form. I was waiting for my burning bush moment, but I couldn't even seem to get a still, small voice. I closed my Bible and went on with my day, frustrated. God had forgotten me.

Waiting for an answer to prayer can sometimes seem like a wasted effort and a long-lost dream. God's timing rarely plays out the way we imagine it should. We begin to think if God would just answer our request, then we could take a step in the right direction rather than wallowing in this paralyzed frustration. We want to do God's will, but we get stuck in a place of unanswered questions and burdens beyond our control. When we are in seasons of waiting to hear a response from God, we often wonder if He heard our request in the first place. But His Word assures us that He does hear. In these silent seasons we have the choice to believe and rely on God or to give way to the doubt that the enemy so clearly sets before us.

Darkness is only a distraction. It does not mean God has departed.

Doubt

I knew God had a plan. I knew this is not the way things would always be; however, questions were starting to fill my mind. Stress was slowly creeping in and filling the restful parts of my soul. Determined to find God's will, as if it were some tangible answer to my prayer, I tried to press forward, but I had no idea where I was going.

We were in and out of the hospital constantly. No one could give us any answers—not the doctors and not God. We waited and waited and waited. Most of my time waiting was on the side of the hospital bed, which is not a bright place—it is a dark, dreaded, discouraging spot for a young mom of three littles.

The pain was overwhelming. I could see it in his heavy eyes. The nurse immediately gave him pain medication. Relief filled my mind as I watched his body relax. I turned away to take a deep breath and heard a knock at the door. The nurse walked in with a long list of questions. I was expecting the normal rundown, but her first question made me wonder if this time we were going to get an answer. "Have you ever had kidney problems?" "No ma'am." "Sir, your kidneys are failing, you won't be going anywhere tonight. We will prepare a room upstairs and transfer you as soon as possible."

Four days went by as I walked the white halls, slept on the blue vinyl sofa bed, and prayed day and night for God to answer our prayer for healing. I watched my husband go from writhing in pain to being completely lifeless, unable to stand up alone. He couldn't walk. He could barely hold a conversation. All the while God was silent.

I made sure Rob was comfortable, and I settled my head on the crunchy hospital pillow and tried to rest. The doctor was making his evening rounds and slipped quietly into our room. Like an out-of-body experience, I watched myself standing like a statue, paralyzed, as he told me that there was nothing more he could do for my husband. No more tests, no more scans, and no more treatment. We were to wait. My face was like a stone and my mind like a freight train rushing into the possibilities of what our future held.

The next day was like a nightmare as I talked to patient advocates, health-care supervisors, infectious disease specialists, and anyone I could get in contact with to try to get answers. With the help of my family and friends, I was able to get my husband transferred to another hospital with a higher level of care. When we arrived in the middle of the night, a team of doctors immediately started tests and evaluations. The doctors continued to come through his room, viewing him like he was a prized case because his condition was so rare. The thirty-year-old man on the sixth floor was dying, but the cause was unknown. The nights were long and lonely as I lay there in that old hospital beside my lifeless soul mate. All the while I wondered what in the world God was doing and why He would not give us an answer.

I began to think the worst. I told God I was willing to walk whatever path He had for us if He would just give us an answer. The pain of the darkness was closing in on me, and I questioned God like I never had before. Have you ever been there? You ask God one thousand questions and wonder why we have to go through such difficult struggles on this earth. I think we've all faced something that brings us to this place. Even though we know where peace comes from, in the midst of our trials, we still question. I'm learning to claim this verse from John when I begin spouting off my list of questions:

> "I have said these things to you, that in me you may have peace. In the world you will have tribulation. But take heart; I have overcome the world." (John 16:33)

What a beautiful promise! He has overcome the world! If only we could remember that when trouble comes knocking.

Three doctors dressed in white entered the room one after the other and closed the door behind them. I can still hear the click as the knob latched into place. They each took a seat around the hospital bed and began to explain that they have not been able to pinpoint what exactly is destroying Rob's body. Then one spoke up. "If the test results continue in this direction, we will have to assume that there is a malignancy." I was no dummy; I knew what malignancy meant, and I began to prepare myself for the worst.

Desperation leads to divine deliverance.

Maybe I could go back to work, get a teaching job, and live with my parents until I could get on my feet. I began to think of a funeral, and I buried Rob every day in my mind. I made myself crazy thinking of all of the possibilities. We did not even have a diagnosis, and yet in my mind I attended my husband's funeral day after day. Isn't it horrible how we always think the worst even when the facts aren't in place for the outcome we imagine?

When we go through seasons of struggle and answers don't come, it is so easy to shake our fists at God as if we deserve an answer, a remedy, a solution. I had my moments in my living room and hospital hallways when I looked up to the ceiling and told God, "I can't understand. We've done everything You've asked us to do. We have given our lives for the sake of the gospel. Now my husband is suffering, and we don't even know what is wrong with him."

We all know that feeling—like life is dark and there's no way out. I don't know what it is in your life, but I do know there are things that are tough and things that we cannot understand. Seasons of strife, confusion, heartache, heartbreak—we all have them. Sometimes people will say it's what we do in those dark times that determines the outcome, but I think sometimes it's what we don't do that truly determines the end result. What I mean is this: if I am constantly pushing through, constantly striving more, constantly trying harder to make it, survive, scheme, and get on with the next thing in my life, I am completely missing what God is doing amid the dark times in my life. What if we stopped to consider the purpose of the darkness?

Sometimes it is more about where we are than what we do. What if we could learn to rest in the restless seasons? What if we could learn to let go of the control we tightly hold on to in the times when we can't see tomorrow? What if no matter what happens in our lives, we could turn over control to God and let Him handle it? See, sometimes rather than doing more, we need to do less. I share this not because I know it all and have this darkness thing down but because I have wallowed in the darkness for long seasons wondering why God wouldn't deliver me. Slowly, I'm learning that there is a purpose for each dark season we walk through.

Experiencing God's power and living anchored in Him isn't about doing more to escape the darkness; it's about learning to live fully in the dark seasons when we cannot see tomorrow and making the choice to look beyond what we cannot see into what God is revealing to us. Desperation leads to divine deliverance.

God used the trial of Rob's illness to teach us so many valuable lessons about darkness. The darkness is one of the most vulnerable and valuable places that God teaches His children. I want to share some of the lessons we learned in hopes that you will be strengthened in your own dark seasons.

God Is Still My Strength in the Dark

I know it sounds trite, doesn't it? God gives us something big in our lives. God gives us strength to get through. We tell others and hope they "get it." When I say God strengthened us, I don't mean He made us powerful in such a way that we were not affected by our trials. I don't mean we floated through the hard times without flinching. I mean we fell flat on our faces and had nowhere else to turn. I mean I lifted my voice to God and asked Him hard questions, like, why in the ever-loving world did we have to go through stuff like this?

I called 911 again and let the EMTs into my home with my children huddled upstairs, afraid Daddy might die. I looked to the sky and screamed within my soul, *NO!* I didn't want this. I didn't want it for me, for my husband, for my children, for anyone. But God tenderly let me finish my fit and loved me even still. He gave me strength to pray with my babies. He gave me grace to care for my husband. He gave me friends who cooked for me and brought me cases of Dr Pepper on days when I felt the world was caving in. Hallelujah for cold Dr Pepper!

Whatever your darkness is, God doesn't expect you to rise above it, but He will be there when you are ready to let Him carry you through it. When the waves are high, the wind is heavy, and you feel like you can't take one more moment of it, God is present in it all.

God is our refuge and strength, a very present help in trouble. (Psalm 46:1 KJV)

Wait on the LORD: be of good courage, and he shall
strengthen thine heart: wait I say on the LORD. (Psalm
27:14 KJV)

God Is Still Close to Me in the Dark

Sometimes it is hard to feel close to God when you cannot
see your hand in front of your face. When all you can see is
what you are going through right now, it's often hard to have a
positive outlook on life.

As a source of comfort, Rob and I knocked on my friend's
door and waited for the answer. My precious friend was an
elderly lady from our church. With her perfectly styled white
hair and large bow at the base of her neck, she wheeled her
chair around the door and greeted us with a huge smile. Rob
and I sat on the red velvet couch and listened to her tell about
days gone by. She shared a verse that God gave her when she
was a little girl and the doctor told her she would never be able
to walk again:

It is good for me that I have been afflicted; that I might
learn thy statutes. The law of thy mouth is better unto me
than thousands of gold and silver. (Psalm 119:71-72 KJV)

We sat as tears streamed down our faces. We knew the
Holy Spirit of God came down into that living room and
spoke through a precious woman who was anchored in God's
power. She didn't know all we were going through. But God
did. And in God's power, my precious friend gave us a treasure
from Scripture that would carry us through many months of

darkness. Learning God's statutes or values wasn't something I thought about when faced with the unknown illness, but God used a precious woman who was anchored in God's Word to share His power with us. Day after day I began telling myself, *It is good that I have been afflicted, that I might learn your statutes!*

Maybe you aren't quite ready to say that affliction is good, but when you are ready, God's Word will not disappoint.

God Is Still My Comfort in the Dark

With glazed eyes I made my way to the hospital cafeteria for coffee. One of the men who had transported Rob in the ambulance approached me and with the most compassion I had seen in a long time said these words: "Your husband is going to be OK. I know it." And he walked away. I don't want to get spooky on you, but I know God's power was speaking through this stranger. I could see it in his eyes, and I could feel it from the tips of my toes to the top of my head and beyond. God sent that angelic man in his huge combat boots and heavy coat, with a scar on his face, to remind me that, in my weakness, God was with me and that this was not the end.

When we walk through stuff in our own strength, sometimes we survive. We even become prideful of what we have been through and feel the need to tell everyone everything that we have endured as a means of letting people know we are strong. What if we admitted our weakness? Through Rob's illness I had no choice. I was sleep deprived with no assurance of tomorrow. Weakness was written all over my face. Though my mind knew God would provide, I was terrified of losing my husband and facing this life alone. God proved to me that in my weakest, most vulnerable moments of life, He is enough. He is my comfort. He is my strength.

> It is of the LORD's mercies that we are not consumed, because his compassions fail not. They are new every morning: great is thy faithfulness. (Lamentations 3:22-23 KJV)

God Is Teaching Me Compassion in the Dark

You may never experience health struggles or the abandonment of a person you love, but whatever you go through or have been through, God has a way of using it to help others. Don't waste your darkness. Let God use you to inspire, encourage, and lift up others who face the same situations. If you are still in the middle of the problems, still facing the dark, still waiting to see what God is doing, use this time to get to know the God of the darkness. He is a powerful anchor that will not budge even when it feels like you are drowning. When you link arms with others who need a life raft, you begin to see Him more clearly.

Darkness isn't cause for distress. It's a call to surrender to the Savior.

Look around in your neighborhood, your church, or the place where you work and start asking people how they really are. You'll find a lot of people living in darkness without the anchor that we know. They will never live anchored in His power unless we show them how. It's not a display of perfection or a lack of transparency. It's living the words we read in Scripture, like my elderly friend or the kind EMT with combat boots and a scarred face who spoke hope into heavy, hurting hearts. It's taking the time to stop and speak when the Holy Spirit prompts your heart. It's making the phone call, sending the card, or providing a meal for the person God puts on your heart.

> Finally, all of you, be like-minded, be sympathetic, love one another, be compassionate and humble.
>
> (1 Peter 3:8 NIV)

> For the Holy Spirit will teach you in that very hour what you ought to say. (Luke 12:12)

God Is Preparing My Heart in the Dark

We were comfortable where we were. A good job, great friends, a cute house, and everything we needed. When Rob got sick, God began to work in our hearts. We knew God was moving us on, but taking the steps to actually move seemed impossible considering Rob's illness. But God has a way of working inside the depths of our hearts even when we do not know what tomorrow holds. Little by little we took steps toward obeying God's call.

> And I am sure of this, that he who began a good work in you will bring it to completion at the day of Jesus Christ.
>
> (Philippians 1:6)

God Is Working for Good in the Dark

We may never really know all the good that came from Rob's sickness, but one of the things God did was transition us from one church to another. We packed our bags and moved a few hours south in obedience to a burden God had placed on hearts during our dark season of unknowns. The church God directed us to would be the church my parents attended. What an amazing orchestration of God's providence. God knew we would need those precious days and years together. It was no accident or obscure coincidence. It was God's plan. Through every storm, He knows and sees more than we could ever imagine. Living anchored in God's power in the dark means I believe God truly is working things out even when life is uncomfortable and difficult.

> And we know that God causes all things to work together for good to those who love God, to those who are called according to His purpose. (Romans 8:28 NASB)

After months of questions, sickness, hospital visits, and no answers, we finally received a diagnosis. The doctor had no explanation except, "Rob's illness is not textbook." As the doctor shared the news with us, he said the good news is, "You are going to get better. The bad news is, it is going to take you about six months before you feel like yourself again." And it did take all of six months. But at that point we were both strengthened, armed, and ready for the new season God had for us. I know it sounds so simple when you sum it up in a sentence, but the cold, hard truth is that it was difficult even though we knew

God had a plan. Every moment of loneliness, worry, and wait-ing was a blessing in disguise. It was God's way of making us more compassionate, more understanding, and more obedient in living anchored in His power in our lives. God anchored us in a way we had never experienced before.

I don't know what type of darkness you have walked through, but I know we each have these seasons. For some it's devastating loss; for others it's financial crisis or perhaps personal baggage or abuse that no one knows about. No mat-ter how much darkness has filled your life, God is the God of everything, and He holds the power over every dark thing.

> He has delivered us from the domain of darkness and
> transferred us to the kingdom of his beloved Son.
>
> (Colossians 1:13)

When we feel so alone and so forgotten, God's power is with us. It's up to us to accept the lessons we learn in the dark about His power. When we honor Him as the anchor of our lives, God uses even the darkness to bring Him glory. Darkness isn't cause for distress. It's a call to surrender to the Savior

> So that Christ may dwell in your hearts through faith;
> and that you, being rooted and grounded in love, may be
> able to comprehend with all the saints what is the breadth
> and length and height and depth, and to know the love of
> Christ which surpasses knowledge, that you may be filled
> up to all the fullness of God. Now to Him who is able to
> do far more abundantly beyond all that we ask or think,

according to the power that works within us, to Him be the glory in the church and in Christ Jesus to all generations forever and ever. Amen. (Ephesians 3:17-21 NASB)

God's presence is powerful even in the dark!

Questions to Ponder

1. How have you experienced God's power in the dark seasons of life?

2. How has God used the darkness to draw you closer to Him?

3. Is there an event in your life that you know God allowed so that you can help others through similar events? How did you use that to expand His kingdom?

4. Who do you know that is walking through darkness right now?

5. How will you encourage them?

Praying God's Power

Dear Heavenly Father,

I become impatient and frustrated when answers do not come. I want to hear Your voice and know You are near, but sometimes You seem so far away. The darkness seems to take over, and I struggle in this place of unrest. Please draw me close during my seasons of darkness, and help me know You are with me even in the dark. You know my deepest need and the questions that fill my mind. You know the doubts and frustrations that cause me to feel alone. Please give me peace as I wait for You and wisdom to see what You have for me in each season. Teach me to rest in Your perfect will. Remind me that I am not alone, and show me who I can encourage as I walk through each season of life.

In Jesus' name, amen.

Experiencing God's Presence

The LORD is my shepherd; I shall not want.
He maketh me to lie down in green pastures: he
    leadeth me beside the still waters.
He restoreth my soul: he leadeth me in the
    paths of righteousness for his name's sake.
Yea, though I walk through the valley of the
    shadow of death, I will fear no evil: for
    thou art with me; thy rod and thy staff
    they comfort me.
Thou preparest a table before me in the pres-
    ence of mine enemies: thou anointest my
    head with oil; my cup runneth over.
Surely goodness and mercy shall follow me all
    the days of my life: and I will dwell in the
    house of the LORD for ever.

—Psalm 23 (KJV)

Chapter 4

Power in the Dream

No one is holy like the Lord!
There is no one besides you;
there is no Rock like our God.
—*1 Samuel 2:2 (NLT)*

Sweet Dreams Shaken

Dressed in our best date-night outfits, we hopped in the car and started down the road. It was my thirtieth birthday. We arrived at the five-star restaurant and followed the hostess to the booth. As we each took our seats and gazed into each other's eyes, I was in awe of the way our love had grown over the years. We ordered Dr Pepper and bacon-wrapped shrimp as an appetizer. Perfection! We talked lavishly about our goals, plans, and dreams. It was one of those good talks, when you dream about the impossibilities of life working out and of growing old together. The good vibes were rolling, and I was so thankful to have a husband to celebrate with.

Feeling the vibration of my phone, I assumed the babysitter had a question or an emergency. I could feel my heart beating as I pulled my phone out. When I saw the name on the screen, my heart stopped and sank all in the same moment. Time froze. For the first time in more than twenty-four years, my biological dad was calling me on my birthday—my thirtieth birthday.

I hesitantly answered the phone, trying to keep my volume to a minimum. Holding back tears and looking across the table at my husband in disbelief, I listened as my dad said, "Happy birthday, baby girl. I hope you have a good time."

Sometimes when we least expect it, something from our past is resurrected. Even things we think we have control over resurface and cause us to struggle, wonder, question, and hurt all over again. The anchor of our soul feels ripped from the roots up. Grief strikes the heart, and there's no escaping the feelings that follow. Just when we think we are anchored in God's power and strong, we begin to feel weaker than ever before.

That night I was reminded that even in the middle of making beautiful memories, celebrating life's milestones, and enjoying the beauty of a marriage relationship, the enemy is always at work behind the scenes. With the simple ring of the phone, my dreams were rattled, shaken, and stirred up all over again. I thought I had conquered the abandonment thing.

There was this tiny piece of my heart that made me believe that someday things would be different. Don't we all want what we think is best for us? We know what life is supposed to look like, and we dream that one day we will all live happily ever after. So when life doesn't go the way we think it should, it's hard to wrap our minds around it. We either hold on for dear life to the hope that maybe things will work out or choose not to trust anybody and become bitter at everything and everyone in our lives not living up to our expectations.

Whatever it is in your life that didn't go the way you thought it should, the enemy desires to make you dwell there. He wants to drag you to the depths of despair and make you take up permanent residence. If you've ever conquered that broken dream and moved on, he waits for just the right time to rake you over the coals again and cause you to desire that dream that may never come to fruition.

Our dreams hold the power to control us. Whether they are broken or fulfilled, sometimes they drive our desires and have an impact on our destiny.

God's glory is more powerful than our unfulfilled dreams.

We can end up feeling either successful, accomplished, and fulfilled or broken, bruised, and bitter. There is power in our dreams. If we live anchored and tied to what we think should have been or should be, we will live defeated beneath unmet expectations and imperfection. But if we live anchored in God's power, we will experience God's presence in a way that feels truly like a dream come true. Many will say God's presence is not a feeling, but I have felt God's presence in my life. When my dreams didn't work out the way I thought, God's power has proved that His ways are higher than mine, and His promises are more powerful than an unfulfilled dream.

If we want to experience God's power in our broken dreams, we must learn to embrace the purpose of every dream. Whether it's a fulfilled dream or a broken dream, God has a purpose. When we learn to live in the depths of that purpose, we begin to experience what it's like to live anchored in God's power. For me, it's learning that being abandoned isn't God's curse or punishment for me; it's God's providence and protection. It is knowing God is using my story even now to encourage and uplift a trembling heart from the depths of despair. God has a purpose in your story. We may never get over what has happened, but we can get through it. And we can live anchored in anything we face when we realize the purpose of every dream, fulfilled or not, is God's glory.

> For God, who commanded the light to shine out of darkness, hath shined in our hearts, to *give* the light of the knowledge of the glory of God in the face of Jesus Christ. But we have this treasure in earthen vessels, that the excellency of the power may be of God, and not of us. *We are* troubled on every side, yet not distressed; *we are* perplexed, but not in despair. (2 Corinthians 4:6-8 KJV)

God's glory is more powerful than our unfulfilled dreams. Although emotions might be tender and the pain might feel fresh, God holds the power to deliver us from what we think life should be like. We hold the power within our hearts to live anchored in spite of the despair and trouble that surround our lives.

Hannah's Devoted Heart

There is a woman in the Bible who helps me deal with the dreams that make me struggle. The story of her life gives us an example to follow in seasons of distress. Although her prayer was answered in the way she asked, it's her heart's devotion that compels me to change my own heart. Her devotion to God and pure heart of adoration for her heavenly Father is captivating.

Hannah's Problem

The barren womb is no new epidemic. From the earliest writings of Scripture we see women who suffered the pain of infertility. There were no pills to take, no procedures to perform, and no testing to find out the source of the problem. All Hannah had was empty hands and an anguish-filled soul. Being barren in those days was interpreted as being worthless. She, like many women, had a mother's heart to love but no child to care for. In her heart she desperately wanted a child and desired the fruit of blessing like every woman in that day.

Hannah had to deal not only with the burden of infertility but also with a woman in her life who taunted, provoked, and bullied her because of it. My heart breaks for sweet Hannah and so many women who face the same difficult path. For many it's infertility, and for others it's something else that makes them struggle, wrestle, and desire something more. For you, it might not be the dream to have a child, but maybe it's a happy marriage, a good job, a college degree, successful adult children, or the desire for someone to acknowledge your gifts and accomplishments. If that one thing would happen, then you would feel accepted, adequate, approved.

What Hannah did with her broken dream in 1 Samuel 1 gives us a beautiful example of what we can do. Hannah was not a perfect woman. She, just like us, had the opportunity and maybe even the desire to get even with her offender, but instead she took her problem to the Lord. Not only that, her focus throughout her struggle proves her heart's desire. It wasn't a selfish desperation for fulfillment. Too often we want things to work out for us and for our good, but Hannah's purity of heart reminds us to keep the purpose of our dreams ever before us: God's glory. That's where Hannah's heart was anchored.

Hannah Prayed (v. 10)

It seems so easy, right? Pray, and then things will work out. But it's complicated when you pray and pray and pray and the answers you want to hear from God do not seem to come. The details in Hannah's emotional state give us insight into her heart. What she was feeling relates realistically to our own desperation. The Bible says in 1 Samuel 1:10, "She was deeply distressed and prayed to the LORD and wept bitterly." This distress Hannah was feeling was the ugly cry: the one that billows out from the depths of your soul and contorts your forehead and chin into wrinkles. It's when you lock yourself in the bathroom or closet and drop to the floor and let it all out. Sometimes we hold on so tightly to what we want, we never cry out to God the way Hannah did. There are times to lock the door, press your knees into the carpet, and let it out. Put your name in the place of Hannah's below and imagine what it would look like for you to cry out to God in this way:

"_____ was deeply distressed and prayed to the LORD and wept bitterly." The key is that we don't leave out the final phrase of that sentence: "and prayed to the Lord." So often we take our unanswered prayers and tuck them away because it is too painful to pray about again and again. We don't know how many times Hannah prayed, but this time was the prayer that was recorded because God wanted us to see that it's OK to weep bitter tears. There is so much we can learn from Hannah in the way she dealt with this dream. Devotion delivers us from despair.

Hannah's Promise (v. 11)

Hannah made a twofold solemn vow to God. The first was that she would give her son back to the Lord for life. Imagine that. She was willing to offer her son, the one dream she desired, fully and completely to God for life. The second was a Nazarite vow that he would live a holy and separated life.

The power in this vow is often overlooked. Hannah promised God she would offer her son back to Him if He would only give her what she wanted—a baby boy. The reality in this vow is that Hannah was willing to literally give her son up to the power of God no matter what that meant. For Hannah to make a vow like this proves her unyielding devotion to her dream. The end-all wasn't about having a baby; it was about bringing God glory through the child's life.

So often our prayers are about ourselves and our glory. We want a new home, more children, and a better-paying job so we can have more, do more, and be more. Hannah's devotion teaches us that we must ask in the light of God's glory that He might increase. The prayers we pray would look very different if we asked for things in the light of God's glory rather than our own.

Hannah Prayed (v. 15)

When I think of Hannah's prayer of desperation, I am often drawn back to my own desperate places and challenged with the reality of what she did with her problem. She didn't shout it for the world to hear or gripe at her husband for not being enough for her. She poured "out [her] soul before the LORD." Too often my first phone call when something goes wrong is to my mother or a good friend. I want to get all the details out and let them know how terrible it is that I am going through such a tragic situation. Or I let it simmer inside until I can't hold it in anymore and spout it out over and over again to anyone who will listen. But Hannah knew where to go in her desperation. She didn't cry to Elkanah or a girlfriend. She went to her anchor and poured out her heart.

It wasn't the prayer, the vow, the crying, the words, or the way Hannah prayed that made the difference for her. It was the power of God that she was anchored to that made the difference. There is power in living desperately anchored in devotion to God.

Hannah's Proof (v. 19)

The proof of Hannah's faith is found in verse 19: "They rose early in the morning and worshipped before the LORD; then they went back to their house at Ramah. And Elkanah knew Hannah his wife, and the LORD remembered her." If you need clarification here, the facts are that Elkanah and Hannah sealed the deal. They acted as if they knew God would fulfill their dream. I love the record here that they worshiped God first and then they went and took care of business. So often we get it backward. We do all we know to do in our own power. We read and scheme and work and do, and then as a last resort, we go to God in our desperation and plead with Him for blessings. Hannah knew enough about God's power to reverently worship Him first and then acted in faith believing He would fulfill her deepest desire. The key to Hannah's faith is not found in the way she acted but in the verse prior to her actions. Before she even put feet to her faith, she believed, trusted, and rested in God's power:

> Then the woman went her way and ate, and her face was
> no longer sad. (1 Samuel 1:18b)

Her countenance was lifted before she conceived. This is so vital for you and me. Whatever it is that we are dreaming for God to do in our lives, we must have faith that God is able to fill the void without providing the desired dream. The real power is in the foundation of Hannah's faith—the anchor. When we are willing to pour out our hearts as Hannah did, believing God will lift our countenance, we are ready to prove our faith. Until then, we will only wallow, worry, and wait for God's power in our lives. Living anchored in God's power means we run into His presence as a first resort, not a last plea for rescue.

> *Every dream devoted to God delivers a distressed heart from despair.*

The real power in this story is not in the birth of Samuel; it's in the conception of Hannah's faith. Even if God never blessed Hannah with a baby boy, the fact that Hannah's countenance was lifted before her dream was fulfilled proves that God's power and glory were present in Hannah's life. For you and me and our dreams, the lesson from Hannah is to let God lift us up before we look for the answer. God's presence is the anchor—the answer, the dream. His power is enough for you and for me. Until we can realize that and have faith and firm assurance of His power, we will never live anchored. It's not just saying it; it's living it. It's pouring out our hearts in the quiet of a closet and letting God know we are willing to live devoted, even if the dream is never fulfilled the way we think it should be. Then we will experience God's glory and understand what a dream come true really means.

Hannah Praised (vv. 27-28)

A son was the one thing Hannah desired so desperately, but she freely offered him back to God in praise. She trusted

God. She knew God had given Samuel to her, and she believed God would do what was best with him and for her. Her prayer of praise in 1 Samuel 2:1-10 is not about Samuel. Never once does Hannah mention Samuel or herself in the prayer. She only praises God for all He has done for her. So often we look for God to do for us what we know He can do, but we miss the miracle. The miracle is not in the birth of the baby, although it's beautiful. The miracle is the power of God's presence in our lives. When we dream, pray for, and desire things that seem impossible, we must not miss the one thing that we are really seeking. It's not about the baby or the blessings; it's about the person of God working in our hearts. That's where dreams are fulfilled, because God proves His power by lifting our countenance regardless of our circumstances.

Sometimes our dreams are manifested as goals, relationships, job promotions, getting married, starting a family, excelling at school or work, or growing old together. All of these are wonderful things, but if we miss the power of God in each step, we are missing the power of the dream altogether. Power in our dreams comes when we begin to see the person of God in place of our problems.

Although my thirtieth birthday is one I will never forget, it's given me a new devotion, a new dream—a dream to let God lift my countenance every day no matter what distractions I face. The next time the enemy knocks on my door with a dream unfulfilled, I'll have a prayer of praise on my lips like Hannah's and a promise of God's glory in my heart. I will know that no matter what interruptions life brings my way,

God's glory is enough to fulfill my deepest desire for a dream come true.

My dream now isn't about my biological dad and what he has or hasn't done in my life. It's about my heavenly Father, who has lifted my face day after day and holds me close in moments when the enemy tries to derail me from the dream come true.

There is power in the dream of living a desperately devoted life.

God has a purpose for your broken dreams. When you feel like your dreams are dashed and all your plans have fallen through, pour your heart out to God. You will find a dream come true in the power of God. Every dream devoted to God delivers a distressed heart from despair.

Questions to Ponder

1. What is one dream that you are praying about in this season of life?

2. What dream has been fulfilled in the past?

3. What one thing do you need God to do to lift your countenance?

4. How does Hannah's prayer encourage you?

5. How does knowing God's glory is the purpose of your life change the way you view your dreams?

Praying God's Power

Dear Heavenly Father,

I want to live devoted to You in every dream. I want to trust that You know and will fulfill Your perfect will in my life. There are things I cannot understand, but I'm learning in the good and the bad that You have a purpose. I'm trusting that Your glory will be revealed in my life through the beautiful and through the broken. I want my life to be a display of devotion and undivided deliverance. Give me power to live beyond the dreams and desires of my heart, and help me to be overwhelmed with a desire for You. Anchor me in Your presence so that when the enemy comes my way, I will be ready to let You lift my countenance and live firmly secure in Your glory.

In Jesus' name, amen.

Experiencing God's Presence: Hannah's Praise

Then Hannah prayed:

"My heart rejoices in the LORD!
   The LORD has made me strong.
Now I have an answer for my enemies;
   I rejoice because you rescued me.
No one is holy like the LORD!
   There is no one besides you;
   there is no Rock like our God.

"Stop acting so proud and haughty!
   Don't speak with such arrogance!
For the LORD is a God who knows what you
      have done;
   he will judge your actions.
The bow of the mighty is now broken,
   and those who stumbled are now strong.
Those who were well fed are now starving,
   and those who were starving are now full.
The childless woman now has seven children,
   and the woman with many children wastes
      away.
The LORD gives both death and life;

he brings some down to the grave but raises
    others up.
The LORD makes some poor and others rich;
    he brings some down and lifts others up.
He lifts the poor from the dust
    and the needy from the garbage dump.
He sets them among princes,
    placing them in seats of honor.
For all the earth is the LORD's,
    and he has set the world in order.

"He will protect his faithful ones,
    but the wicked will disappear in darkness.
No one will succeed by strength alone.
    Those who fight against the LORD will be
        shattered.
He thunders against them from heaven;
    the LORD judges throughout the earth.
He gives power to his king;
    he increases the strength of his anointed one."

—1 Samuel 2:1-10 (NLT)

Part 2

Present Power

Chapter 5

Power in My Mind

When I remember You on my bed,
I meditate on You in the night watches.
—Psalm 63:6 (NASB)

Wishful Thinking

I squinted through the dark, looking across the room at the clock, which seemed to never change. The numbers on the alarm clock crept by as I lay awake wishing for rest, relief, and reassurance.

Have you ever experienced something so consuming it kept you awake at night? Fear, doubt, anger, or unexplained issues cluttered your mind as you desperately desired rest. Your body was exhausted, begging for sleep, but thoughts continued to bombard your mind faster than you could process them as you looked at the ceiling, flipped side to side, and tried to find the perfect spot on the bed for sleeping. Finally you closed your eyes and begged God to help you sleep. But your mind would not cooperate.

It's not surprising we have a hard time telling our minds

to shut down when they continue to churn thoughts out repeatedly. "The average person has about 48.6 thoughts per minute," according to the Laboratory of Neuro Imaging at the University of Southern California. "That adds up to a total of 70,000 thoughts per day."[1] Think about that for a minute. Every day our minds are constantly processing things we see and experience. What if in the midst of all those thoughts we could experience God's power in our minds, and what if God's power could override the thoughts that keep us awake at night?

One of my favorite psalms when I can't sleep is Psalm 63.

> O God, You are my God; I shall seek You
>   earnestly;
> My soul thirsts for You, my flesh yearns
>   for You,
> In a dry and weary land where there is no water.
> Thus I have seen You in the sanctuary,
> To see Your power and Your glory.
> Because Your lovingkindness is better than life,
> My lips will praise You.
> . . . .
> When I remember You on my bed,
> I meditate on You in the night watches,
> For You have been my help,
> And in the shadow of Your wings I sing for joy.
>
> —Psalm 63:1-3, 6-7 (NASB)

David wrote this psalm in the dry wilderness of Judah. In our seasons of spiritual drought, when we experience sleepless nights and the power of God feels far away, we, like David, have a place to go—a place filled with power that anchors us when we would otherwise drift into the depths of despair. But sometimes it's hard to know how to get back to that place where we once felt anchored and secure. In this chapter we will identify the causes of our struggle and learn a new way of processing thoughts from our problems into God's power.

I want to live free from the trap of constantly recycling the hurts and regrets that seem to run through my mind like a rushing freight train. It's time for us to put it to rest. No longer do we have to produce anxious thoughts that don't reflect the power of God. We can overcome these thoughts and learn what to do when our minds begin to wander into seasons of anxiety. This is exactly what Paul talks about in Ephesians 4:23 when he says, "Be renewed in the spirit of your mind" (NASB). As we learn how to renew our minds through God's power, we will realize we no longer have to stay in the same place of turmoil.

The thoughts that keep us awake at night or give us that gnawing feeling deep inside our guts usually fall into one of four categories: love, life events, loss, or lies. If we can identify these thoughts, label them, and replace them with truth from God's Word, we will be able to experience the power of a mind

> When we shift our focus to Jesus and His love, acceptance, and forgiveness, we begin to realize the love we truly desired all along.

anchored in God's presence. When any of these issues begin to threaten our thought patterns, we can be assured we have a new way to deal with them.

You can experience God's power as you process your thoughts into these areas by naming rather than ignoring what you are feeling and uncovering which areas of life trip you up the most. Once you are aware of the thoughts overpowering you, it will be much more likely that you can gain freedom in your thoughts through the power of God. Here are the areas I believe many of our thoughts fall into.

Love

Love encompasses relationships with family, coworkers, neighbors, friends, and everything in between.

I can still feel the piercing glare as she looked at me across the lunchroom. I remember the feeling of knowing that someone I trusted said something about me behind my back. I knew what was said wasn't true, but other people didn't. I got home that night and let the hurts of my heart gush onto the page of my journal. The next day I took out my journal again and poured out the day's dilemmas and dramas thinking that maybe, if I wrote every ounce of anger on paper, I would feel better. With every problem I encountered, I would take out my journal and reread again what happened yesterday, last week, and the weeks before that. And just in case I ever forgot the wounds inflicted, I had a record I could go back to. And I did. I relived the scenarios of hurtful wounds over and over.

It might sound elementary or immature to rehash wounds, but sometimes as an adult I replay unkind words said to me. I don't write about it like I did in junior high, but I think about it. I recall my facial expression when the words were said and wonder if my reply should have been different. My mind replays what I wish I had said if only I could have thought a little quicker in the moment. But I didn't. So now I let it seep, simmer, and steal my sleep. It's not the best way to process my thoughts, but it seems to be the place I always go, and it leaves me feeling powerless. Have you ever been there, rehashing the words said or wanting desperately for things to have worked out differently?

As long as we continue the same thought process when we encounter situations in relationships, we will continue rehashing old wounds and inflicting more pain. Power in our minds comes when we stop the same old strategies of either avoiding conflict by internalizing everything, hoping time will resolve the problems (therefore never facing them), or worse, pretending it never happened until the issue comes up again and old memories cause us grief. It might feel good to get it out on paper, post a passive-aggressive comment on social media, or tell a friend about it with the nitty-gritty details. But by the time you lay your head on your pillow, you'll be replaying the words you said and wishing you had said it differently—or said nothing at all. I know this to be true because I have endless journals filled with heartaches, but my journal never healed me of my pain. It only gave me a record to replay the pain. By continuing to focus on the way I was hurt or the person who hurt me, I am pulling away from the One who keeps me anchored.

Our minds can only be filled with God's power when we focus on the one relationship that holds everything we truly need. When our relationship with Jesus is weak or nonexistent, we will continually reach for anyone on this earth who will give us a sense of worth. We begin to feel desperate for someone to give us a thumbs-up. When our worth is put into question by a relationship that didn't end well, our thinking is affected, and the power in our minds is immediately compromised. All of our feelings and thoughts become focused in the wrong direction—on the person who hurt us or on ourselves. When we shift our focus to Jesus and His love, acceptance, and forgiveness, we begin to realize the love we truly desired all along. We will find healing when we anchor our thoughts by focusing on our relationship with Jesus and the way He unconditionally loves, pursues, and forgives rather than the broken relationships on this earth. There will still be the need to walk through conflict and learn through mistakes, but when we keep our focus on Jesus, we are able to navigate those treacherous waters of difficult relationships.

Living anchored in God's power in our minds means we live today with a renewed focus on Jesus, and we start on a new path by filling our thoughts with Him instead of ourselves: what we've done, what we've heard, what we've said. Picture the day ending on your thoughts—like a sunset—and not being able to go back to that day. Another thing you can do to change the path you are on is refuse to rehash old wounds and choose to focus on the people who are present in your life today. When you don't make this choice, you lose time with the people you love. When we begin to change our focus and fix our eyes on Jesus' unconditional love, we will discover it's all that really matters. And we will gain strength through His power.

Life Events

If we could sit for a while and chat about life, I would ask you where you grew up and what life was like as a child. I would want to know about your dreams, your deepest struggles, and how you made it. We all have those things that have happened to us and seem to define us. So when we are asked a question like, "How did you get to where you are?" the answer is

> What you have experienced has the potential to be the springboard of experiencing God like never before.

complicated. It's a mix of so many different life events that it's hard to sum it up in one sitting, isn't it?

Along with those life events, there are victories, regrets, and broken parts of life that make us who we have become. It seems anytime I talk to someone about life, it's the hard things that stand out as having impacted who we are, how we live, and what we do. Those hard life events consume our thinking. It's one thing to learn lessons from the hard parts of life, but it's a completely different thing to be locked into a life of yesterday.

Making a change when it comes to the way we view our life events is complicated. If we've always thought of ourselves as a victim or a failure because of what has happened in our lives, it's hard to get around it and discover a new way of thinking. If you will stick with me through this process of change, I think you will begin to see the key that unlocks our overcrowded minds. The only way for us to make a change is to allow the Holy Spirit to first identify the problem. For example, I was abandoned. As I process this event, it's easy to take on a victim status. I was left behind and rejected by a person who was supposed to keep me safe. I could continue to dwell on this event and relive the sting of rejection, but I've learned there is a better way to live. Rather than focusing my emotional energy and time on the facts of my childhood, I have learned to focus my attention on the facts of my heavenly Father. He loves me. His love makes me victorious. He is for me and wants to be close to me. When I set my mind on this rather than the facts of the past, I am able to begin to live anchored in the present. It doesn't change what happened to me, but it frees me from restless nights of mental bondage. You too can find freedom from those things that seem to bind you. As we identify the problems in our lives and shift our focus from our problems to God's power, we begin the process of living anchored even amid the difficult events of life.

Loss

I love music. It's one of the most therapeutic things I have ever experienced. One of my favorite things to do when I am home alone is sing at the top of my lungs and dance like no one will ever see. But there was a season of silence in my life—a season when it was hard to sing. In the depths of my heart I wanted to, but baggage from loss I had experienced filled my mind. I couldn't lift my voice like I used to.

When we lose something or someone we love, it fills us with a void in our minds so big that sometimes we don't even know how we got to where we are. We change. We don't necessarily want to change, but loss impacts us greatly, and life becomes different. When we try to pretend that we didn't experience loss or try to think our way into a new season of life, we end up short every time. We continue to grieve, and it begins to feel as if we will never get better. There is hope for these seasons of life, but we will never find relief in our own attempts at positive thinking or hoping time will eventually heal the hurt. Time doesn't heal all wounds; Jesus does. As we begin to identify these areas and face the truth of what we have endured in our lives, we need to come to the realization that Jesus is the only way to transformational thinking, especially when it comes to loss.

As you deal with loss in your life, know that it is OK to grieve. Sometimes when we lose something or someone, we think life will never be the same. The truth is, it won't. But that does not mean life can never be good again. Your life can be good again. What you have experienced has the potential to be the springboard of experiencing God like never before. When we face loss, we have a choice to trust God or not. When we choose not to trust, we live powerless, pain-filled lives searching for relief in all the wrong places. When we choose to rely on God as our comforter and healer and dwell on His power, we can be renewed and comforted. Eventually we will be able to help someone else experience the same comfort. It's not that we forget the loss or even leave it behind, but we are propelled by the security we know we have in Jesus. You can have that security, healing, and comfort. But you must focus your mind on Him.

> You will keep him in perfect peace
> Whose mind is stayed on you,
>> Because he trusts in you. (Isaiah 26:3)

I love the use of the word *stayed* here. Other translations use the word *steadfast*, meaning "unwavering." As we continue this journey of identifying the areas where we need to make changes, consider one of the biggest changes in your life sits on the brink of how steadily you focus your mind on Christ. When your mind is fixated on Jesus and your thoughts are filled with trust and faith that He will do what He says, you will learn what it means to lived anchored in God's power.

Lies

The final area that will often trip us up the most, keeping us from experiencing God's power, is lies. The devil is labeled the "father of lies" in John 8:44, and we would be foolish to avoid this topic when it comes to our thinking. I don't know about you, but this one is a daily battle. It's not that I'm a pathological liar, but the devil is, and he often tries to deceive me with his subtle attacks through his lies. He tells me I'm not a good housekeeper, mom, or wife. He plants seeds of doubt about my adequacy and competence in my daily tasks. He's constantly trying to undermine any spiritual victory by convincing me life is all about me. When we believe his lies, we become entangled in a sticky web of believing we can't do anything right.

Have you ever thought you weren't good enough to complete the task? You look around and see other people much more qualified. Their achievements seem excellent, and yours seem average at best. So you hustle and work harder. We are often chasing a lie from the devil that we need to do more to be more, and to achieve more in order to be accepted more. It's false. You are enough with Jesus. If we could simply grasp hold of the truth of Jesus' redemption and victory over sin, we would begin to live anchored like never before. But issues arise when we take the bait as Eve did in the garden. "Did God really say that?" "Can God really fill your mind with His power?" Sometimes in the name of spiritual exploration, we, like Eve, take hold of a lie through doubt and questions. Jesus does not condemn you and say things like, "You're not good enough" or "You'll never succeed." Jesus says, "If you abide in my word, you are truly my disciples, and you will know the truth, and the truth will set you free" (John 8:31-32).

Power in our minds comes when we embrace the truth of God's Word rather than the lies of the devil. That's when we will be set free from the lies that hold us back. We will be able to rest our heads after a long day and close our eyes in calm assurance that Jesus forgives us when we mess up. He loves us when we don't get everything just right. We can know that

His power is the only thing strong enough to truly sustain the attacks of the enemy.

Once we realize the four areas that jeopardize God's power in our minds—love, life events, loss, and lies—we are ready to make changes in our thinking that not only impact our lives but those around us as well. As we pinpoint the areas the enemy wants to destroy, we will begin to recognize his attacks before we are deceived. We hold the power through the Holy Spirit to experience conviction. Don't be afraid of conviction. Conviction is a red flag, a whistle, a warning sign that something isn't right. Embrace it and experience the power of the Holy Spirit.

Experience God's Power

As we walk through the steps on the following pages, they might sound simple, but applying them tends to be a challenge. I promise, if you will take one step at a time, you will be well on your way to living anchored in God's power in your mind, and it's a beautiful place to live. It's a place of freedom and sweet sleep. Are you ready? Here we go!

Pray over it.

The first thing we need to do to experience power in our minds is pray. It sounds so Christian, so "good." Right? But I'm learning that if I never exercise what I say I believe, my belief is more like an idea. If we truly believe there is power in prayer, and we don't pray to God about the things that consume our minds, we are forfeiting the opportunity to experience God's power. Prayer is essential to transforming our minds, and yet so often we wait to pray until there is no other option. We let sleepless nights roll on and on with no real communication with God. Eventually we give in, bowing our knees that have buckled and collapsed to the ground.

If I don't pray, I won't experience God's power. Prayer really is the key to unlocking the power of God in our minds. Asking God to reveal the truth of what is consuming you is one of the most powerful things you can do. For me, I often have allowed issues of love, life events, loss, and lies to control everything about my life. I focus on those issues as if life is all about them. God continues to teach me that as long as I keep my mind on my life and the things that happened to me, my power is limited to my own strength. And it is never enough. I need His strength and His words for my life, not my own.

Identify it.

If we really want to experience God's power in our minds, the second thing we must do is identify the controlling thought patterns that sabotage our minds. If we never identify the problem, we will never make a change. Remember how many thoughts we think each day? More than seventy thousand. It seems nearly impossible to truly bring every one of those thoughts to God, but if we can identify the ones that cause us distress and ask God to reveal the truth, we will see God's power in our minds as we hear the truth from Him.

If I don't identify the problem, I won't experience the power. Identifying the thoughts we need to change and finding out which area of life we struggle with the most is vital. Without identifying the problem, there is no changing the thought pattern. It's not enough to just identify it; we must continue with the process and embrace step 3.

Obey.

The third thing we must do is obey God's instruction. No matter what our lives looked like in the past or look like today, we all have the same opportunity to change the way we experience God in our minds when we obey Him. Without taking God's Word as truth and obeying what He says, we won't understand Him and the power He offers. Paul gives us the key to obedience when it comes to our thoughts. "We destroy arguments and every lofty opinion raised against the knowledge of God, and take every thought captive to obey Christ" (2 Corinthians 10:5).

Any thought that isn't from God must be taken captive and identified. Once we give it a name (love, life events, loss, or lies) and know that it's not from God, we cannot stop there. Obedience to Jesus is an essential step to complete this idea of captivating the compromising thought. How do we obey? How do we know what to do next? We must understand what God's Word says about obedience.

In Scripture, obedience is always tied to blessings. Truth is tied to freedom. Understanding is tied to wisdom. Trust is tied to direction and guidance. Faith is tied to revelation and miracles. Obedience is so much more than following a list of rules. It's deciding in your mind that you choose Jesus over the problems of this life by trusting and having faith in Him. It's deciding to stop the thoughts you know God didn't place within your mind and replacing them with truth. It's choosing life-giving words over gut-wrenching ones. Obedience is a vital key to power in your mind. When we don't trust God at His word, we are living in disobedience. And yet we wonder why we can't sleep. When we want to remember the wrong that was done to us one more time, we aren't choosing to obey and taking every thought captive. We are literally saying, "No, God. I don't want Your power. I want to feel my pain one more time." What does this mean for you and me today? It means we have a choice to experience

> *Transformational thinking comes when we see truth instead of trauma.*

God's power in our minds. We can choose to do what we've always done, or we can choose to obey Christ. Power resides in choosing obedience, and we apply it in the next step.

Stop it.

When I get out my journal and remind myself of the hurtful words spoken and the exact tone in which they were said, I am continuing in my same old ways. At some point we have to admit that rehashing the hurt isn't helping. It's like a bad habit that takes time to change. The first thing you do when you want to quit drinking soda or biting your nails is make a choice. It's the same here. Then we need to act on that choice and daily make the decision to stop the thoughts that continually cause us anxiety. But it's hard. Paul understood our struggle. He said, "For I know that nothing good dwells in me, that is, in my flesh. For I have the desire to do what is right, but not the ability to carry it out. For I do not do the good I want, but the evil I do not want is what I keep on doing" (Romans 7:18-19).

Isn't that the way it feels sometimes? We want to have power-filled minds and wisdom to overcome the thoughts that bombard our thinking, but we continually go back to our same old ways. We could throw up our hands in frustration and tell God, "See? Even Paul couldn't get it together." But just a few verses later Paul gives us a nugget of truth that is life-changing. He says, "For the mind that is set on the flesh is hostile to God, for it does not submit to God's law; indeed, it cannot. Those who are in the flesh cannot please God. You, however, are not in the flesh but in the Spirit, if in fact the Spirit of God dwells in you" (Romans 8:7-9).

Did you catch that? The mind that is focused on the world and its heartaches is completely disobedient or "hostile" to God. Wow! That's such a strong statement, and it deeply convicts my heart. So often I am consumed with what is happening in my life rather than living consumed with God. If we want to live an anchored life full of God's power, we must ask the Spirit who dwells in us to help us stop our destructive thought patterns. How do we do it? We stop the thought in its tracks and replace it with the truth of Scripture. Let's explore this more in the next step.

Replace it.

Replacing the old thought with a new one is essential to controlling those intrusive thoughts. Sometimes we like to replay the things that have happened to us because it makes us feel justified in our anger or our hurt feelings. But as long as we replay it, we cannot replace it.

Replacing the old thoughts with truth from God's Word looks something like this:

When we remember the sting of a relationship that ended, God's Word says:

> I will never leave you, nor forsake you. (Hebrews 13:5)

When we feel betrayed by someone we trusted, God's Word says:

> It is better to trust in the LORD than to put confidence in princes. (Psalm 118:9 KJV)

When we don't understand why, God's Word says:

> Trust in the LORD with all your heart, and do not lean on your own understanding. In all your ways acknowledge him, and he will make straight your paths.
> (Proverbs 3:5-6)

When we think we can't make it, God's Word says:

> Do not fear, for I am with you; do not anxiously look about you, for I am your God. I will strengthen you, surely

I will help you, surely I will uphold you with My righteous right hand. (Isaiah 41:10 NASB)

When we think no one understands what we are going through, God's Word says:

God is our refuge and strength, a very present help in trouble. (Psalm 46:1 KJV)

When we think the loss is too great and we will never recover, God's Word says:

My flesh and my heart may fail, but God is the strength of my heart and my portion forever. (Psalm 73:26)

When we think there is nothing good to look forward to, God's Word says:

In the world you will have tribulation. But take heart; I have overcome the world. (John 16:33b)

When we don't feel loved and can't understand why life is so hard, God's Word says:

For God so loved the world, that he gave his only Son, that whoever believes in him should not perish but have eternal life. (John 3:16)

God's Word is the power source that fills our minds with truth. We take a thought and line it up with Scripture. God's Word becomes the power we use to break destructive thought patterns. Take another look at the truth in the verses above.

Which truth does God want you to use to put in the place of an old thought that has held you captive for far too long?

When we hold to truth and replace those old, musty thoughts with God's Word, we begin to discover the miracle of His power in our minds. We will be able to forgive the person who hurt us deeply because we will see his or her brokenness through the lens of God's forgiveness and mercy. We will experience comfort in the seasons of life when nothing is going right because we will have the presence of God to carry us through. His Word steps in when thoughts threaten our peace. Power in our minds can seem impossible to attain, but it's not. It's available, and it's accessible. You can experience God's power in your greatest struggle when you choose to let Him fill you with truth.

Transformational thinking comes when we see truth instead of trauma.

Questions to Ponder

1. What problems are consuming your mind that you can't let go of?

2. Identify within each area the specific problem you struggle with most.

   Love:

   Life events:

   Loss:

   Lies:

3. Considering the things you mention above, which step of
   the process is hardest for you?

   Pray over it.

   Identify it.

   Obey.

   Stop it.

   Replace it.

4. What change can you make today to begin the process of
   experiencing God's power in your mind?

Praying God's Power

Dear Heavenly Father,

I need Your divine power in my mind. I know I am not strong enough in my own mind to stand against the attacks of the enemy. Please help me fill my mind with Your Word and Your power. Give me specific Scripture to memorize and tuck so deeply into my mind that when the enemy looks my way, I will be ready. When I begin to think I know what's best, remind me that I need You most. As I seek You daily in my mind, give me wisdom to think thoughts that are true, holy, and right. Give me power in my mind.

In Jesus' name, amen.

Experiencing God's Presence

My soul clings to the dust;
    give me life according to your word!
When I told of my ways, you answered me;
    teach me your statutes!
Make me understand the way of your precepts,
    and I will meditate on your wondrous works.
My soul melts away for sorrow;
    strengthen me according to your word!
Put false ways far from me
    and graciously teach me your law!
I have chosen the way of faithfulness;
    I set your rules before me.
I cling to your testimonies, O LORD;
    let me not be put to shame!

—Psalm 119:25-31

Power in My Heart

*I pray that God, the source of hope, will
fill you completely with joy and peace
because you trust in him. Then you will
overflow with confident hope through
the power of the Holy Spirit.*
                    —Romans 15:13 (NLT)

Cheer Me On, Pretty Please!

I had prepared an amazing blog series, and I was so excited to post it. I was sure that it would get a ton of traffic and that my girlfriends would be calling to tell me what an amazing word from God it was. God had given me specific words, and I knew without a doubt that I was supposed to post the series. It was one of those "God moments." I mean God came down into my living room and gave me the words, the verses, everything.

I typed and worked and made it look the best I knew how. Then it came time to post. I checked, double-checked, and checked again just to make sure there were no typos or words that sounded out of place. I held my breath and clicked "Post."

There it was, posted online for the entire world to see, my revelation from God. I waited for the amazing response. In my mind, a word from God meant this post was going viral! I could not wait to see how God was going to make it happen!

Silence

I sent a text to one of my best girlfriends and asked her to take a look and let me know what she thought. I was sure she was going to give me rave reviews. Waiting anxiously, I stared at the phone and double-checked to make sure I typed my text correctly. My heart beat fast as I waited for my phone to buzz at any moment. I waited, and nothing. No text, no call, not even a little thumbs-up emoji.

Immediately I started developing thoughts of why she didn't respond. *She must think my calling is a waste of time. Even my best friend isn't reading my blog. Maybe it is a waste. She didn't like the idea of my post at all. She probably thinks I'm being ridiculous for putting my words out there for all the world to see.* Defeated, discouraged, and irritated, I put my phone to the side and pouted.

The Games We Play

Late that night, she finally sent me a sweet, encouraging text. By that time, though, I had already decided that she hated the post, so when I read her actual words, I had a hard time believing them. I convinced myself that if she really meant what she was saying, she would have replied earlier. So of course I did what any normal girl would do, and I didn't respond. I mean, if she could wait all day to respond to me, I did not need to respond to her right away. Before you start throwing stones my way, I know you've been there too. Maybe it wasn't a text, but perhaps you've withheld a hello or a hug. Maybe you wanted to say something nice, but jealousy or envy snatched away your desire to encourage. Maybe you've jerked away from your hubby, thinking he only wants one thing from you, when all he really wants is your attention and affirmation. We all fail, friends. Let's go ahead and link arms and decide we aren't going to throw rocks at each other. It's not really worth it.

> *A focused heart brings simplicity and satisfaction to life. A divided heart brings discouragement.*

My dear friend never intended to hurt me. She did not even do anything that qualified me labeling her actions as hurtful. The only thing I had to accuse her of was the timing of her text. Later, I found out that she had actually had a very busy day with her family and did not have time to stop her entire world for a five-hundred-word post that I thought everyone in the world should read.

To me, the five-hundred-word post was important, my word from God. I was sure that it would be a big help in everyone else's life too. There are many times in my life that I have to learn to stop trying to please people and focus my heart solely on God. This was one of those times that God taught me to stop focusing on the approval of others and let Him be enough for me. Yes, God gave me the words to share. Yes, God told me to post it for the world to see. Yes, God was in control of the timing of who would see it and how they would be impacted. So many times we take control, thinking we know best, when God is calling us to leave the details up to Him. In my own power I become frustrated, irritated, and even irrational when I don't see the results I want. But when I live with an anchored heart in His power, I live secure in God's timing, God's purpose, God's provision, and God's plan. Even if I don't get the approval of my best friend right away.

Whose Approval Do I Need?

I allowed something God-given to become man-driven. Don't we all have these moments? We want to see results. We want to know that our mothering, our marriage, our working, our goal setting, and our dreaming will amount to something. We want tangible results that we can cling to, and when our names aren't attached to the things God is calling us to, it starts to feel like maybe we heard God incorrectly. But we didn't. What we did do is get our hearts looking in the wrong direction. Rather than focusing on the Father, we begin focusing on our own favor. No wonder it feels so wrong when this happens. Our hearts get flustered and we wrestle with how things are working out and who is getting the credit for what. The disciples knew this feeling. The words Jesus says to Peter in John 21 pierce my heart with deep conviction when I get my heart fixed on myself and begin to worry about who gets the credit for what.

Peter turned and saw the disciple whom Jesus loved
following them, the one who also had leaned back against
him during the supper and had said, "Lord, who is it that
is going to betray you?" When Peter saw him, he said to
Jesus, "Lord, what about this man?" Jesus said to him, "If it
is my will that he remain until I come, what is that to you?
You follow me!" So the saying spread abroad among the
brothers that this disciple was not to die; yet Jesus did not
say to him that he was not to die, but, "If it is my will that
he remain until I come, what is that to you?"

(John 21:20-23)

Jesus is letting Peter know that the important thing is following Jesus with singleness of heart. Sometimes we get so
wrapped up in who is being called to do this, who is moving where, who is staying put, who is embarking on that, or
who failed at their latest endeavor. All along, Jesus is saying the
same words to us as He did to Peter: "What is that to you?"

Each of our lives has a specific, uniquely designed purpose.
Until we allow God to speak directly to our individual hearts,
we will be seeking the approval of friends, focusing on everyone and everything else except for Jesus. When we look to Him
with all our hearts, He is constantly saying, "Follow me."

The Necessary Habit: Focus

"True success happens when no one is looking, when
no one hears, in the quiet of your heart where there's only a
divine invitation and an acceptance of it."[1] A focused heart

brings simplicity and satisfaction to life. A divided heart brings discouragement.

It is hard to admit that we have divided hearts. It is not what we desire, but somehow we easily fall into the trap of seeking everything and anything except God and His power. How are we supposed to completely rely on God's wisdom and strength each and every day with friends, family, and life pulling for our attention at every turn? When the Holy Spirit speaks, His voice is drowned out by the noise of life that seems to fill up every inch of space. It's no wonder we can't feel Him nudge our hearts.

A heart with a single focus on the Father is a heart that finds the favor of God. We all want God's favor, but living in it seems tough, especially when we don't know how to access it. When we do experience God's favor, we often dwell in the moment. We think we must have done something right to deserve His attention and entirely miss the point of God's presence. God's power is not something we achieve in order to flaunt. It's a discipline we bow to and a surrendered state of being we live in. Living with an anchored heart full of power is a continual seeking of the Savior even after we've found Him. The more we seek Him with all of our hearts, the more we find Him. The more we find Him, the more we feel Him near.

> You will seek me and find me, when you seek me with all
> your heart. (Jeremiah 29:13)

As we continue this journey of living anchored in God's power, walk with me through three simple keys to living with a focused heart. You may not think your heart is away from God, but we all have moments just like I did with my friend. We hear from God. We want to share it. Then we look for the results. We want to see what God is going to do with our obedience. Results and rewards are the driving force of our culture. We are always looking for the next "like" or recognition. We become desperate for a thumbs-up or the approval of others so much that we are willing to pay for more "likes" and the perception of approval. Living with an anchored heart is about keeping the focus on the Father instead of on our own favor.

Three Ways to Focus Your Heart

"You shall love the Lord your God with all your heart and with all your soul and with all your mind."

(Matthew 22:37)

Focus on the Goal: God's Presence

The goal of an anchored heart is living in constant rhythm with the beat of the Father. It's knowing that God's presence is the result of living anchored and tethered to Jesus. It's listening intently to the voice of the Holy Spirit and knowing He will answer anything we ask in faith with wisdom, grace, and mercy. A focused heart is so firmly anchored that there is no wavering when the wind of success, fame, or fear of failure blows in. It's not about winning in the world's eyes. It's about living without the delusion of desiring approval from people. The world's ways will constantly have us seeking satisfaction in success. God's way involves learning that true success is a surrendered heart fully focused on the Father. Living in God's power involves learning that success has nothing to do with what we do, achieve, or accom-

plish, but it has everything to do

A forgiven heart is a power-full heart.

with who we love, listen to, and lean on. As long as we live with a divided heart, we will never experience the power of an undivided heart—the place God's power resides.

Ask yourself these questions to evaluate your current goals:

> What do I want to do with my life?
> What accomplishment will make me feel accepted and successful?
> Who am I trying to seek approval from right now?

The truth is God *does* equip us with gifts, talents, and abilities, but those gifts *are not* given for us to feel worth or worthy. Those gifts are given for one purpose: that the Father might be glorified.

Power in our hearts never comes with what we do or accomplish or whose approval we gain on earth. We waver and miss out on God's power because we focus on the gifts we possess and not the goal of God's presence. Success is birthed when we realize that true power from the Holy Spirit is only found when the goal is God's presence rather than man's stamp of approval or praise.

Find Forgiveness: Embrace Change

Most people do not enjoy change. Once you break in a pair of shoes or jeans, it's hard to break in new ones. I find myself reverting back to my old, faithful, comfortable favorites. We do the same with our success. When we hear the applause, the compliments, and the approval of people, we feel accomplished and accepted—comfortable. Change is hard, but if we are going to live with anchored hearts, we must learn to let go of the praise of man and cling to the power of God. Life might not look as glamorous from the outside, but the internal benefits are beyond beautiful. Eventually what is on the inside will come out, and it will not matter what anyone thinks or says. What will matter is that your heart is clean and pure and full of power.

To prepare for change we must find forgiveness for anything that has caused division in our hearts. We must say like David:

> Search me, O God, and know my heart!
> Try me and know my thoughts!
> And see if there be any grievous way in me,
>   and lead me in the way everlasting!
> (Psalm 139:23-24)

When we ask God to reveal the sin in our hearts, we are taking a huge step toward His power. A forgiven heart is a power-full heart. Once the sin is removed, change can happen. As long as we hold on to those old, comfortable patterns of seeking approval and rubbing shoulders with the people that always give us a thumbs-up we will never experience a power-full heart free from the bondage of sin.

Fear Not: Live with an Anchored Heart

We often let our hearts get all wrapped up in the problems of our lives and forget that God offers us the power of protection and peace.

> "Let not your hearts be troubled. Believe in God; believe also in me." (John 14:1)

After we make the choice to follow Jesus, we receive an amazing gift. It's an eternal gift that we so often forget about, and we press on in our own power, wishing for something more. We have it! We have the more! It's up to us to believe it and rest in it.

> "And I will ask the Father, and he will give you another Helper, to be with you forever, even the Spirit of truth, whom the world cannot receive, because it neither sees him nor knows him. You know him, for he dwells with you and will be in you." (John 14:16-17)

Just as Jesus proclaimed to the disciples that the Holy Spirit of truth would be with them, we have the same gift. The Holy Spirit is the most personal, closest part of the Trinity that we experience on this earth. While Jesus is the sacrifice for our sins, the Holy Spirit sends the conviction so that we know we need to be forgiven. It's the Holy Spirit who reveals sin in our hearts. It's the Holy Spirit who prompts our hearts to surrender.

It's the Holy Spirit of God who provides protection, provision, and peace. Jesus said it this way:

> "But the Helper, the Holy Spirit, whom the Father will
> send in my name, he will teach you all things and bring to
> your remembrance all that I have said to you. Peace I leave
> with you; my peace I give to you. Not as the world gives do
> I give to you. Let not your hearts be troubled, neither let
> them be afraid." (John 14:26-27)

When we choose to accept the promise of power through the Holy Spirit's presence in our hearts, we are choosing to embrace the promise of power. As long as we search for power in other places, we will consistently be looking for acceptance in all the wrong avenues, striving to feel something magical or accomplish something amazing. God's power gives us the miraculous without any of our doing as a requirement. When we experience the peace of His power, we will begin to understand that it's not in what we do that delivers us. It's what He has already done. God's power provides the heart with everything it needs. The presence of God's Spirit within us is enough to satisfy our deepest desire for acceptance and success.

If we want to experience God's power, we must surrender to the Spirit that lives within. This means we listen when conviction pricks the tender spots of our being. It means we give in and say, "Yes, Lord, I'm sorry. I need you. Forgive me. Be with me. I'm listening. I love you." Too often we rush around and expect God to follow us. Yes, He promises to never leave or forsake us, but His command is constantly the same:

Abide in Me.
Hear My words.
Obey My voice.
Be still.
Know Me.
Follow Me.

God's power in our hearts is more than knowledge in our heads. It's an undivided desire to know the Holy Spirit, who lives within the believing heart. God's presence allows us to find forgiveness and anchor our hearts in His power.

Questions to Ponder

1. What causes your heart to be divided?

2. Where do you regularly seek approval from others?

3. What sin has God revealed in your heart that needs to be forgiven?

4. How can you change your focus to live a more power-full life?

5. When was the last time you know the Holy Spirit convicted or comforted your heart?

6. What gifts has God given you to use for His kingdom?

Praying God's Power

Dear Heavenly Father,

I want to live an undivided life. I want my heart to be so clean before You that I have no reason to be ashamed. Forgive me when I fail and reveal my sin when I am blinded by my own desires. Give me fresh eyes to see Your grace and goodness in my heart. When I avoid conviction, help me embrace it and see my need for You more clearly. Give me the desire to please You in everything I do, and free me from the feelings of needing acceptance from the world around me. When I get distracted and begin my own striving for acceptance, remind me of Your power in my heart.

In Jesus' name, amen.

Experiencing God's Presence

O LORD, you have searched me and known me!
You know when I sit down and when I rise up;
  you discern my thoughts from afar.
You search out my path and my lying down
  and are acquainted with all my ways.
Even before a word is on my tongue,
  behold, O LORD, you know it altogether.
You hem me in, behind and before,
  and lay your hand upon me.
Such knowledge is too wonderful for me;
  it is high; I cannot attain it.

—Psalm 139:1-6

Chapter 7

Power in My Life

*But you will receive power when the
Holy Spirit has come upon you, and you
will be my witnesses in Jerusalem and in
all Judea and Samaria, and to the end of
the earth.*

—*Acts 1:8*

Our Words

They prepped my adoptive dad for surgery, and we waited. Just weeks before, we had received news that no one ever wants to hear: "It's cancer." So many emotions bombard your heart when you hear these words. It's not always a death sentence, but sometimes it feels that way. Even though treatments are advanced, the unknowns begin to crowd your mind, and the struggle in your heart begins.

The nurse came in and out of the room, filling out paperwork, checking his vitals, and chatting about sports and life. We had a good time laughing and joking about anything and everything we could think of. You would never know he was getting ready to go through a major surgery. Then Dad did what he always does, and he asked the nurse, "Do you know Jesus?"

The room was still, the laughter stopped, and she turned and said, "Hmm?"

"Do you know Jesus?"

"Oh." She chuckled. "Yes, I know him."

"Do you know Him as your Savior?" Dad asked again.

She laughed again as to keep the tone light. "I know Him," she said.

She carried on and began joking as a way to keep things comfortable. As I sat there and listened to my dad ask the nurse about her relationship with Jesus, I struggled in my heart. The surgery my dad was about to endure would be a traumatic surgery, and I wrestled to understand why God would allow it. You see, my dad was about to get a cancerous lesion removed from his tongue. One-third of his tongue would be removed in order to get all the cancer. I could not understand why God would allow this particular type of can-

Power present in a person's heart reveals hope to a hurting world.

cer to affect a man who was consistently using his mouth to edify, glorify, and spread the name of Jesus. Why wouldn't God preserve his mouth, protect it, and allow my dad to continue using his boldness to glorify God?

A pastor from our church entered the room just as I argued with God in my heart, and he read these verses aloud:

Hear my cry, O God; attend unto my prayer. From the end
of the earth will I cry unto thee, when my heart is overwhelmed: lead me to the rock that is higher than I. For
thou hast been a shelter for me, and a strong tower from
the enemy. (Psalm 61:1-3 KJV)

Often when we are overwhelmed and cannot understand
what God is doing, we desire to hear from Him, and we want a
message written in the sky. We need that confirmation that He
is near and that He is aware of all that we are going through.
God proved to me in that moment that although my dad was
facing a rough road ahead, God's presence was more powerful
than anything we would go through. The shelter of His presence
surrounded me, and the strong tower protecting me from the
devices of the enemy comforted me. The devil waits for the moment when our hearts are most tender, raw, and undone, and he
creeps in subtly with questions, fears, and doubts. If he can get
us to forfeit the power of God in our lives, he knows we will live
in turmoil throughout the tragedies of life. But God's power is
stronger. By the simple reading aloud of His word, my heart was
pierced with conviction, comfort, and a deep calm knowing God
was in complete control. God securely settled my shivering soul.

We may never know why God allowed my dad to go through
head and neck cancer, but we do know God's power prevails no
matter what the world brings our way. You may wonder how
people have faith through the tough stuff of life. I'm learning
that living anchored in God's power is the only way. God's power
present in a person's heart reveals hope to a hurting world.

I don't know if the nurse who chuckled at the name of Jesus truly knows Him, but I do know this: she's heard His name, she's seen His hope through the faith of a hurting man, and she's experienced God's peace in a pre-op room where His presence was evident. Power in our hearts isn't reserved for a church service or a Damascus Road experience. It's available right now by simply speaking the name of Jesus or quoting the words of Scripture. We never know when we will lose the ability to speak His name. So say it! Speak up. Be bold like my dad, and ask people if they know Jesus.

It might feel awkward or uncomfortable, or perhaps even offensive. But my dad reminds me often that the name of Jesus is offensive because it holds the power over the enemy. When our hearts are filled with God's Word, God's Word flows from our mouths. When we speak His words, we experience His power in our lives.

> "And when they bring you before the synagogues and the rulers and the authorities, do not be anxious about how you should defend yourself or what you should say, for the Holy Spirit will teach you in that very hour what you ought to say." (Luke 12:11-12)

Our Actions

She leaned in close and whispered, "I don't know what I'd do without you."

"I don't know what I'd do without you either." I replied.

My eight-year-old daughter loves art, and we happened to have a few minutes to color together. Nothing fancy, just a princess coloring page with a scene of trees and sky. I picked up the green crayon. She picked up blue, and together we colored.

When she leaned in with her precious words, I asked her, "What made you think to say that?"

Her response was candid and clear: "I just like coloring with you."

When we spend time doing the things we love with the people we love, we feel connected and valued. We gain a new appreciation for the things that our loved ones value, and we begin to value it too. When I sat down to color with Madalyn, I didn't imagine this would be a moment for making memories, when time would freeze and the beauty of blue and green crayon would forever be sketched in my heart. But it was. It was a precious heart treasure that I will never forget. There's something powerful about the intentional moments we spend together with the people we love.

The same is true with God. When we spend undivided time with God doing the things God loves, we begin to learn the value of a devoted life. While coloring with Madalyn, I chose to put my distractions aside and focus. There are plenty of times when I try to multitask and end up messing things up by causing stress and drama with the people I love the most. But this time God taught me something

Once we change the way we look at the power in our lives, we will change the way we look at everything.

beautiful as I held the crayon carefully and stayed inside the lines, filling in the white space with my complete attention on the task at hand. When we try to fill the white space in our lives with more than God and get distracted with everything going on around us, we miss the opportunity to see the masterpiece God is making right before our eyes. Madalyn didn't want to talk or play or have me watch her; she wanted me to color with her. Sometimes rather than doing so much for God, I just need to get my heart in tune with His and be with Him. Power in our lives is not so much something that is produced as something that is practiced. It's a discipline of fewer distractions and more devotion.

Too often we are so distracted by everything pulling for our attention that we look here and look there and miss the miracle of the moment. Misguided by the things we see or hear or want, we press on in our own power and wonder why we end up feeling powerless.

Paul talked about it like this: "the lust of the flesh, and the lust of the eyes, and the pride of life" (1 John 2:16 KJV). When I think of those three things in regard to my own life, I like to think I have it down. Who wants to believe the truth about oneself being a creature of lust or pride? It's difficult to even type these words. I don't like admitting that my flesh has desires that are sinful, but it's true.

My pride is always the sneaky one. It creeps in and deceives me into thinking that I somehow can produce power in my life in my own strength. Here is what pride looks like in my life: "You are a good mom for coloring with your daughter."

Maybe it's true, and maybe it's not a bad thing to think. I mean, who wants to think of herself as a bad mom? And coloring with her was great, right? But when I dwell on this thought and glory in my coloring victories or home-cooked meals, I am taking all the credit for the power in my life.

What if I could change my way of looking at the victories from "I'm a good mom" to "God is so gracious to help me love my children." It changes the subject of the matter from me to He. When our focus is on God and His strength, our lives are full of power. When our focus is on self, our hearts are full of pride.

This is a lesson I need every single day. Once we change the way we look at the power in our lives, we will change the way we look at everything. We will begin to see God's power in everything we encounter, and it is a beautiful display of His presence.

Our Motives

He looked up at me with sincere concern. "Mom. What if she's faking?"

Holding back the tears and smiling calmly, I shook my head. "She's not, sweetie."

The facts appeared obvious. She was in a casket, lying lifeless, but in his six-year-old mind, he questioned the reality of the situation. We've probably all been there, standing by a casket, staring intently, looking for an eyelid to twitch, a finger to move, or a chest to rise with life. Or perhaps my family is the only one who thinks these crazy thoughts. Regardless, we are faced with the same question in our spiritual lives. In the same naive way that Jaxon asked the question at the funeral, we must take a long, hard look at ourselves and ask ourselves, "What if I'm faking?"

We learn quickly how to put on a happy face and pretend life is good. We learn how to bow our heads and lift our hands. We learn to say, "I'm praying for you, and God is good." But living in God's power is more than raising a hand in a worship service or saying a word of blessing in God's name. Power in our lives is the living, breathing Word of God within us. It's the Holy Spirit working through our words, our actions, our motives. It's genuine and sincere, and it convicts our hearts when we are faking.

Sometimes we wonder why we feel powerless in the quiet of our own souls. Or in front of others, we feel empowered as long as people seem to like what we have to say. But when the lights go down and no one sees, what then? Have you ever lain awake at night asking God, "Where are you?"

It's time to welcome God into your everyday life. Not for the moment of despair or the crisis that cripples you, but for the simple moments of coloring with a child. God's power was with Madalyn and me in that simple moment. If we miss God in the little things, we will never experience His power in the lavish things.

When it's my turn to get prepped for surgery and I feel the weight of life on my shoulders, I pray I will be able to genuinely live anchored in the power of God like my dad, saying, "Do you know Jesus as your Savior?"

We can't continue faking power when we don't know what it's like to experience God. God is present today. Right now. In the midst of whatever your life holds. From rocking a baby to ordering dinner at a drive-through window or putting the trash out on the curb, God is there in you. We must stop pretending, stop practicing the right words, and start preaching the name of Jesus. When His Word falls fresh from our mouths, freely from our hearts, and sincerely from the depths of our souls, that's when we'll know God's power is with us. His power compels us to love others so much that we can't help but tell them about His presence in our lives.

> "A new commandment I give to you, that you love one another: just as I have loved you, you also are to love one another. By this all people will know that you are my disciples, if you have love for one another." (John 13:34-35)

> For the desires of the flesh are against the Spirit, and the desires of the Spirit are against the flesh, for these are opposed to each other, to keep you from doing the things you want to do. (Galatians 5:17)

As you learn to navigate a life anchored in God's power, I want to provide you with five truths from God's Word that will help guide you when your life feels less than powerful because of the problems you face. Before you read these, I want you to embrace the fact that no matter what life looks like or has looked like in the past, these powerful truths are God's valuable gift to you for today. Right now, in the midst of whatever you face, these words of power are yours to embrace, hold on to, and live by.

Some of them are comforting, some convicting, but they all hold the same promise—God's power is the anchor of life.

5 Promises of Power in Your Life

For God has not given us a spirit of fear, but of power and of love and of a sound mind. (2 Timothy 1:7 NKJV)

"For the Holy Spirit will teach you in that very hour what you ought to say." (Luke 12:12)

For I am not ashamed of the gospel, for it is the power of God for salvation to everyone who believes, to the Jew first and also to the Greek. (Romans 1:16)

Therefore, since we have been justified by faith, we have peace with God through our Lord Jesus Christ. Through him we have also obtained access by faith into this grace in which we stand, and we rejoice in hope of the glory of God. (Romans 5:1-2)

Such is the confidence that we have through Christ toward God. Not that we are sufficient in ourselves to claim anything as coming from us, but our sufficiency is from God, who has made us sufficient to be ministers of a new covenant, not of the letter but of the Spirit. For the letter kills, but the Spirit gives life. (2 Corinthians 3:4-6)

Questions to Ponder

1. How has Jesus changed your life?

2. What part of your life have you tried to fake?

3. Recall a time when the Holy Spirit gave you words to say, but you hushed Him and didn't share His power with someone.

4. Have you experienced God's power in the mundane moments of your day? Describe what this looked like.

5. When you think about God's power in your life, what is one thing you can do today to experience His presence?

Praying God's Power

Dear Heavenly Father,

I want to experience Your power in my life. There have been seasons where I've faked it and tried in my own strength to press on. I want to surrender every day to Your power in my mind, my heart, and my life. I want to know that no matter what I go through in my life, You will be with me. I want to share the power You provide with others. Give me the words to say and the wisdom to say it. I need Your power, and I desire Your presence more than anything in this world.

In Jesus' name, amen.

Experiencing God's Presence

He who dwells in the shelter of the Most High
　　will abide in the shadow of the Almighty.
I will say to the LORD, "My refuge and my
　　　fortress,
　　my God, in whom I trust."

For he will deliver you from the snare of the
　　　fowler
　　and from the deadly pestilence.
He will cover you with his pinions,
　　and under his wings you will find refuge;
　　his faithfulness is a shield and buckler.
You will not fear the terror of the night,
　　nor the arrow that flies by day,
nor the pestilence that stalks in darkness,
　　nor the destruction that wastes at noonday.

A thousand may fall at your side,
　　ten thousand at your right hand,
　　but it will not come near you.
You will only look with your eyes
　　and see the recompense of the wicked.

Because you have made the LORD your dwelling
　　　place—
　　the Most High, who is my refuge—

no evil shall be allowed to befall you,
    no plague come near your tent.

For he will command his angels concerning you
    to guard you in all your ways.
On their hands they will bear you up,
    lest you strike your foot against a stone.
You will tread on the lion and the adder;
    the young lion and the serpent you will
        trample underfoot.

"Because he holds fast to me in love, I will
        deliver him;
    I will protect him, because he knows my
        name.
When he calls to me, I will answer him;
    I will be with him in trouble;
    I will rescue him and honor him.
With long life I will satisfy him
    and show him my salvation."

                —Psalm 91

Part 3

Potential Power

Chapter 8

Power in Position

How lovely is your dwelling place,
   O LORD of hosts!
                                        —*Psalm 84:1*

Security on the Seashore

The waves were crashing high, and I could taste the salt in the air as I watched my children jump each wave. The fun they were having radiated through their smiles, and the excitement exploded with each new current. As the tide carried them a little farther out into the ocean, my natural instinct was to call them back to me. I hollered out each name, thinking they would be able to hear me. But they continued to jump and frolic and play. I called again, a little louder. Concern filled my heart as I watched the waves slowly carry them farther from shore. I stood up from my beach chair and walked into the water, calling their names and waving my arms frantically, like a crazy person. Finally, they heard me and headed toward shore.

When they were within a safe distance, I sat down. A while

later my oldest came and sat down beside me. My heart was a little more relaxed knowing she was safe. No waves to crash into her, no tide to pull her away, no salt to get into her eyes. She was close and secure.

Sometimes we get busy jumping in the waves of life. We frolic and play and work and do until we eventually look back toward the shoreline and see that we are farther away than we ever intended. I imagine Jesus on the shore with arms open wide, saying my name and calling me back to Him. There is safety when I am close to Jesus.

> *God doesn't need us to be good enough; His grace is enough.*

Even if the waves crash farther up the shoreline, I am still safe when I choose to be near Him.

We Forget

The problem we often run into is that we forget our position in Christ. We forget that He cares for us in dark times even though He has carried us time and time again. We forget that He loves us unconditionally. And we forget that no matter what happens in life, we are in His care. We get distracted by life and get carried into the depths of the sea. Difficult things come into our lives, and we begin to struggle to hear His voice. The waves are too loud. The wind is too strong, and the sound of His voice is drowned out in the distance. Sometimes we catch a glimpse of Him, but we enjoy jumping in the waves.

You Are His Child

If you have put your faith and trust in Jesus Christ, you are His child. He watches intently as you do this thing we call life. He sees and knows every wave that threatens to take you under. He knows when a tsunami is going to burst into your world and rock it until you have nowhere to turn. He cares for you like a mother who holds her precious newborn for the first time. He knows every single hair on your head—and the true color of it. He is your heavenly Father, and He loves you unconditionally. He does not enjoy seeing you struggle. He wants to rescue you and save you and walk with you.

If you have never trusted Jesus as your Savior and Lord, won't you do that today? Simply put your faith in Jesus. It's simply believing He is who He says He is—that He came as a baby, was killed as a man, and rose again as a king who now lives in heaven and waits for you to join Him when you die. Your position as His child is not something you were born with. You have a free will and a choice to make. If you are struggling beneath waves of doubt and confusion about your position in Christ, it is time to run into His open arms. Now is the time to pray a prayer of belief in Him. Ask Him to come into your heart and life. You can experience God's presence right now, no matter where you are or have been, and no matter what you have been through or done. God sent Jesus as the sacrifice for the sins of every person on this earth. He doesn't condemn you or damn you to a life of struggles. He promises to give you peace and comfort every single day.

"For God did not send his Son into the world to condemn the world, but in order that the world might be saved through him." (John 3:17)

Blessed be the God and Father of our Lord Jesus Christ, the Father of mercies and God of all comfort, who comforts us in all our affliction, so that we may be able to comfort those who are in any affliction, with the comfort with which we ourselves are comforted by God.

(2 Corinthians 1:3-4)

When I become uncomfortable in life because of what is happening around me or because I feel the need to accomplish something more, I immediately resort to what I know makes me feel comfortable. I look to what I know how to do well, quickly forgetting all about my secure position and comfort in Christ. I begin to find worth in what I can do in my own strength and power and completely forget who I am in Christ. Instead of resting securely in my position as God's child who has been redeemed, forgiven, and set free from the bondage of this world, I wrestle in my own strength to accomplish something that seems good to me and forget about God's power in me. And there I strive, wrestling with my human will to be good enough for God. God doesn't need us to be good enough; His grace is enough.

Sister / Sister

I have a heart sister in the Bible. Her name is Martha. She gets me. She is a type-A kind of woman with a little sass.

While her sister Mary bows and worships the Lord, Martha is whipping up a good, hot dinner. Martha wanted to be good enough and do enough to make Jesus proud of her. She wanted him to see all she could do to please Him. She wanted Jesus to see that she was willing to work her tail off for Him. She wanted the details and ambiance to be perfect for Jesus. And Mary, well, she chose to sit down at the feet of Jesus. Although Martha's efforts seemed needful and good—purposeful, even—Jesus tells the ladies that Mary had chosen the best thing: worship. The food wasn't important, neither was the color of the tablecloth or the details in the spread of the feast. What was good was that Mary was willing to rest in the grace and goodness of Jesus' presence. Sitting with Jesus is more important than sacrifice of self. Mary's position physically implied her belief in the power of Jesus, and our position proves our belief too.

Kara Tippets puts it beautifully: "My going, doing, loving was my faith, not my nearness to Jesus. In my mind I knew my efforts weren't the substance of my faith, but my practice betrayed me. Stripped of my ability, I saw Jesus in a new and profound way."[1]

Sitting Is Not on the List

If you are anything like me, it is difficult to sit when there are things that need to be done. My list of to-dos is always long. The things on the list never end, and I feel like I am always losing the ongoing battle of getting things done. On top of that,

I have burdens that are heavy. Trials, troubles, and struggles come in tides too high to ride alone.

Sitting down just to sit is not something that I include on my list. I rarely have a moment to simply sit. If I do sit for any period of time, I usually grab a book, a notepad, or my computer and get to work on the long list of things to accomplish.

Completed tasks bring feelings of success. What most of us miss is the same thing that Martha missed. We get so busy "doing" that we do not even think to sit at Jesus' feet—the very place we first met Him and knew His power. When we stop long enough to notice our surroundings, we see someone else bowing before the Lord. Our minds are immediately filled with thoughts about what they should be doing and how they should be doing it. We pride ourselves in our own good works and continue in our busyness that we think makes us spiritual. All the while we wonder why God's power won't rest on us but seems to be resting on them.

Priscilla Shirer's words from her book, *Discerning the Voice of God,* pierce my heart with conviction in my own pursuit of seeking God's power:

> We think all of our bustle and busyness in the pursuit of
> Christian living somehow makes Him more likely to speak
> to us once He recognizes how hard we're willing to work
> for him. From that perspective, stopping to listen to Him
> in order to make room for His guidance sounds bland and
> ordinary. Too easy. Uneventful. A waste of time for people
> who can get as much done as we can.[2]

He saved us, not because of works done by us in righteousness, but according to his own mercy, by the washing of
regeneration and renewal of the Holy Spirit. (Titus 3:5)

We often look at our accomplishments and those of others and compare notes. If our accomplishments look good, we
feel satisfied with where we are and settle into the comfort of
what we are doing. We are much like my children jumping
the waves. We are aware of those around us but cannot really
hear or see what is happening on the shore. We are insecure,
but we frolic in our own foolish, self-created security. True
security comes when I sit with my Savior. That's where I find
my anchor.

Martha, Be Still

The church is full of Marthas. You'll see them everywhere.
They volunteer, fill open spots, attend every event, rush to fill
needs, and have a sense of worth in their work. Before you get
angry and think I am criticizing volunteers of the church, you
should know that the only reason I can describe Martha so
well is because I fight every day not to be her. I am naturally
wired to be a Martha. I don't like sitting on the shore. I want
to be in the deep water, doing something.

Stillness is difficult for me. Sitting seems like a waste. Until
we can fully grasp the reality of the few words that Jesus spoke
to the women that day, we will never stop long enough to truly
worship Him. We might see Him in the distance with arms
open wide, but we will not hear His voice as we so desire. We

will never experience the power of sitting anchored in God's power until we stop chasing after good works.

I have sat in church services, conferences, and teaching sessions time and time again only to have my mind filled with what I need to do to help clean up, prepare, tear down, or teach. My mind has a difficult time slowing down enough to focus on the message and digest the words that are being taught. I long to hear the Word of God, and I want to learn; but my mind wanders, my desires drift, and my grocery list calls my name very loudly. The still, small voice of the Holy Spirit is easily drowned out. This is what Martha was dealing with. Mashed potatoes, fried fish, and apple pie spoke success to her. Sitting with Jesus was too simple. How foolish we are to view success through Martha's eyes. Mary chose the good part, the part that looked unnecessary or wasteful to Martha. The key to Mary's position was the discipline it took to sit.

> *True security comes when I sit with my Savior. That's where I find my anchor.*

Sometimes I feel like a dog in training that just needs another treat or blessing to be reminded to sit. As soon as God proves His presence, there I go bowing down and lifting my hands. Before I know it, I'm pressing on again just like Martha until I'm hit with another wave of His power. Down I go on my knees. I wonder sometimes if God is up there shaking His head, saying, "Micah, stay." It takes discipline to learn to sit, but more than that, it takes devotion. The power in Mary's heart was not about the discipline of her life but the devotion of her heart. Rather than waiting for God's power to bless us, we need to worship the all-powerful God. That's when we will understand the power in our position.

I Can Do What I Want

Standing tall, the determined toddler climbed from her high chair and embarked on her quest for freedom in the crowded restaurant. She had that crazy look in her eyes as if she was about to conquer the world, and she took off. She ran fast, deliberate laps around our table. She circled once, twice, and kept going and going as fast as she could. I thought surely she would tire out soon or crash into someone or one of her parents would snatch her up and buckle her down. But that didn't happen. She ran and ran. Eventually she got off course and took off to the back of the restaurant, her dad running after her.

Looking back on this situation, I think we are all a lot like that little girl. We stand up tall and climb to our destination of choice. It looks fun and rewarding. We take off and run and run and run until we see other things that grab our attention. And then we run some more. It takes our Father's correction before we realize that the path we are running was never meant for us. How foolish we can be when God has to get up from His seat and rescue us from the deep water of our own doing. How different our lives would look if we simply lived anchored in our position with our heavenly Father.

How do we sit confidently on the shore with Jesus without running and jumping in the waves of life? I am learning that when I sit with Jesus, He carries me through the waves no matter how deep or how high. It is not that I never face difficult times or never question why things occur. But when I know my position in Christ, I can be confident, comforted, and calm through the deepest water I have ever experienced, and I can do the work He calls me to and find rest in the power of His presence. I am His child, and He is my Father. When I live anchored in my position, I no longer frolic through waves insecurely or wrestle with doing too much or too little for the kingdom. I live anchored, secure, and satisfied in the presence of the anchor of my life, Jesus Christ.

You're Trying Too Hard

Your day might begin with the pitter-patter of little feet, with a long commute, or after a sleepless night. We all have things that challenge our schedule and our strength. When we make excuses and allow the distractions of life to fill every moment, we become like Martha. We glorify the busyness of life and allow our schedules to become overbooked and crowded. Time at Jesus' feet becomes impossible. How is a person who is booked from dawn to dusk going to have time to sit? They aren't.

We must learn to eliminate distractions. Whether you have a busy work schedule or are busy at home, there must be time for sitting. If you are a scheduler, maybe you should mark it on your calendar, but you will struggle with it if you view it as another task to check off of your list. That will defeat your entire purpose. To spend time at Jesus' feet, loving him and worshiping him, we must have hearts that are focused on Him continually. Put away your calendar, your list, your phone, and any other device that threatens to distract you, and be alone with God.

Children, media, lighting, noise, and undone responsibilities all threaten to pull us away from our anchor. We have to be alone with God and protect our time with Him. Sometimes it means getting up early before the other people in our homes to intentionally avoid distractions. Then we must commit our hearts to God's desires and His presence in every moment. It is not easy to sit still, but when our position becomes clear in His presence, we realize the anchor of our lives is worthy of our worship. We have to learn to make provision in order to experience God's power.

I feel productive when I work. I feel peace when I rest in His presence. Which do I need more? Do I need to be productive? Is that what gives me worth? Is that what God wants from me, to produce more? Has God called you and me to production or to peace? When I rest in Him, I feel something completely different from what I feel when I am busy doing things. His presence fills me with the acceptance that I need so much that my work no longer gives me identity.

For many years I identified myself with what I did. Think of how people introduce each other.

"This is Joe, the firefighter."
"This is Mary, Jesus' mother."

"This is Sue, the pastor's wife."

"This is Lori, Ella's mom."

"This is John, the Baptist."

With every introduction, there is usually a title, job, or affiliation that accompanies the name to identify the person. It's natural for what we do to identify us. I have never heard anyone introduced as a worshiper. Can you imagine?

"Good morning, friends. This is Wanda, the worshiper."

No, we don't identify with that. But according to the Bible, Jesus says, "Mary has chosen that good part, which will not be taken away from her" (Luke 10:42 NKJV). That part is worship. The unspoken value is priceless. The unspoken power is peace.

There will be times when we need to decide what distractions need to be eliminated from our lives so that we can experience God's power personally. What is it that needs to be stripped away to be able to sit at the feet of Jesus without work filling your mind, comparisons crippling your thoughts, and distractions pulling you away? Jesus never said to do, do, do. He said, "Follow me." Overdoing will only leave you overdone.

Sit at His Feet

As I slowly opened the back door, I immediately felt compelled to go to the altar. I had stood in countless services and wanted to pray at the altar, but with people watching, I was filled with the fear of being seen. I did not want people to assume I was confessing a hidden sin or worshiping God like a hypocrite, hoping people would see my display of spirituality.

> The fear of man bringeth a snare: but whoso putteth his trust in the Lord shall be made safe. (Proverbs 29:25 KJV)

But on this occasion, it was different. Our church had opened its doors for twenty-four hours of prayer and worship. Skeptically, I decided I would go for prayer. It was not an event but rather a place to worship. No one stood at the front and directed; it was just an open room. A man was playing a guitar and singing. People were scattered throughout the room. The sight was one I had never experienced before. Some people were kneeling, others were sitting, crying, praying, some hands were lifted, and some hands were folded.

In this type of atmosphere, one that was created for you to come as you are and go as you please, I literally felt like I could have run to the altar. No one was there to be seen, and no one was there to see me. I did not need to worry about who was watching or if they would see me shed a tear. I just knelt. I placed my phone, keys, sunglasses, and Bible on the altar, and I wept. Words did not come, but I felt God's presence there. I lingered. Yes, I have had similar moments in my living room, pressing my knees to the floor, but there was something about going to the church where I had heard God's Word preached and taught. The same place I had wanted to kneel week after week as God's Word pierced my heart, I finally did without the snare of what people would think holding me back. I cried without the concern of my flesh being embarrassed, evaluated, or judged by curious onlookers. No service. No show. No preaching. No teaching. No snare. Just a longing heart positioned expectantly at the feet of the Father.

As I recall the drive to the church that day, I drove fast. Although my mind wondered what it would be like, something deep in my heart was calling me. The tears come even now as I remember walking the aisle to kneel. In slow motion, I placed my things on the altar, and I cried. God knew why I came. Not to be seen but to see and to sit, to acknowledge my position as His. The gift I received from Him was the power of His presence.

If we are ever going to experience God's presence, we must stop our busy schedules and assume our rightful place. Drive fast to where He is and stay awhile. I think Mary would tell us to stop doing so much, stop trying so hard, stop wishing for the next big gig, and just be alone in His presence. There is power there. When you see the face of God, the peace is indescribable. You might think I sound crazy as I speak about seeing God. It's not a physical form I speak of. It is a holy presence that surrounds my being. He is real, and He is present. His arms are open wide, and He is waiting as the most powerful anchor you will ever experience.

If you don't feel close to Him, ask Him to reveal Himself to you. Stop allowing the current to pull you farther away, and assume your rightful position with your Father. His arms are waiting for you. His love is freely offered to you. His comfort is always available for you. His power is ever present with you. Living anchored with Him is the most powerful place you will ever experience.

Questions to Ponder

1. Are you fighting or frolicking in the waves? Describe how that feels.

2. What would you need to change in order to sit on the shore with Jesus?

3. What in your life is distracting you from God's presence?

4. How can you be alone with God today?

5. Have you felt God's presence? Record your experience here.

Praying God's Power

Dear Heavenly Father,

Oh, how I wander away in my own foolishness. When hard times multiply, I feel insecure. I try to take things into my own hands, and I make a mess. I get far away, and the water gets way too deep. I want to be close to You. I want You to carry me, and I want to hear Your voice. God, please help me stay close to You. Give me peace as I draw near to the shore, and give me hope when the waves start crashing around me. Hold me. Lift me. Carry me. I worship You. I honor You. I am Your child, and I know You are my Father. Thank You for never leaving or forsaking me. Today, Jesus, I sit at Your feet.

In Jesus' name, amen.

Experiencing God's Presence

How lovely are Your dwelling places,
    O Lord of hosts!
My soul longed and even yearned for the courts
    of the Lord;
My heart and my flesh sing for joy to the
    living God.
The bird also has found a house,
And the swallow a nest for herself, where she
    may lay her young,
Even Your altars, O Lord of hosts,
My King and my God.
How blessed are those who dwell in Your
    house!
They are ever praising You.   *Selah.*
How blessed is the man whose strength is
    in You,
In whose heart are the highways to Zion!
Passing through the valley of Baca they make it
    a spring;
The early rain also covers it with blessings.
They go from strength to strength,
Every one of them appears before God in Zion.
O Lord God of hosts, hear my prayer;
Give ear, O God of Jacob!   *Selah.*

Behold our shield, O God,
And look upon the face of Your anointed.
For a day in Your courts is better than a
    thousand outside.
I would rather stand at the threshold of the
    house of my God
Than dwell in the tents of wickedness.
For the LORD God is a sun and shield;
The LORD gives grace and glory;
No good thing does He withhold from those
    who walk uprightly.
O LORD of hosts,
    How blessed is the man who trusts in You!

—Psalm 84 NASB

Chapter 9

Power in Perspective

Incline Your ear, O LORD, and answer me;
For I am afflicted and needy.
—Psalm 86:1

The Beauty of a Bruised Banana

The bananas sat on the kitchen counter, brown and bruised from little hands that tried to help carry in the groceries. A normal family might toss them in the trash can after a couple of days or put them in the freezer for future use, but I have a member of my family who loves a brown banana. It's not that he likes a mushy one or one that is overripe, but he has learned that just because a banana is brown and bruised does not mean it tastes bad. He likes the ones that are not as green because he knows the brown ones contain sweeter fruit. The bruised bananas have not been handled as carefully as the flawless ones—they have been through a little more trauma.

Sometimes in life it is easy to see the bruises and the hard times and not ever really experience the sweetness beyond the struggle. Our eyes get accustomed to the difficult things, and all we see is tragedy, pain, heartache, struggle, tears, broken-ness, and loneliness. The fruit or sweetness seems so distant and impossible.

What if we could look beyond the bruises and the way life has been handled roughly and see fruit in our lives? Is it possible that everything that happens, even the bad things, can be used for God's glory and purpose? I believe it is possible. God has a purpose in the pain. We may not see His plan, and we may not completely understand, but God has a plan in all things to bring glory and honor to His kingdom.

When we realize our position as His child and are con-fident in our purpose to glorify Him, we can then begin to shape our perspective on life. If we produce our perspective before laying the foundation of our position in Christ, the focus will be skewed and mis-construed. There is no way to have a proper perspective with-out first finalizing our position.

Perspective is providential.

Until we have a relationship with Jesus and follow His lead-ing, we will not be able to see the fruit of His power in our lives. The veil of understanding and knowledge is lifted when we submit to His wisdom and ways. Without submission, we cannot see clearly.

If only we could all look at the bruises of life and realize the sweetness that lies beyond the outer circumstances, then we would be able to walk through the darkness without fear of destruction, failure, or the future. Although the banana may hold scars, it still bears sweet fruit. As we walk through hard times, I propose to you that fruit is being produced. Yes, there will be scars. There will even be pain. But the product God is forming is beautiful.

When life is bananas, there will be bruises. When there are bruises, there will be pain. When there is pain, it is so important to keep track of your perspective. How you look at your life will determine how you think, act, and live. Perspective is providential.

A proper perspective does not mean life will be easy, but it does mean you can have hope. When you view your life as an eternal one as God's child, there is the hope of heaven. When life is viewed as earthly, there is turmoil of tomorrow. God says, "Take no thought of tomorrow." God says, "I know the plans I have for you." God says, "No one can pluck you out of My hand." God says, "I will never leave you or forsake you." God says, "I give you hope." God says, "My power will come upon you."

No Escaping

I stood at my kitchen stove in a trance. The heat from the pan slowly lifted to my face. Children were buckled in high chairs waiting to be fed, and I was hoping to make it through another day without a complete meltdown (from me or the kids). My life seemed simple in my mind, and yet my emotions were extremely complex.

I could not decipher exactly what I was feeling, but tears seeping down my trembling face seemed like my normal. I didn't like to cry. I hated it actually. It gave me a headache that would last the entire day. Trying to escape the emotional turmoil that filled my mind in that moment, I recalled a verse. With confident resound I spoke aloud these words:

> For God hath not given us the spirit of fear, but of power
> and of love and of a sound mind. (2 Timothy 1:7 KJV)

I breathed a heavy sigh and heard a tiny voice behind me say, "I want that sound mind." As if my toddler really knew what I needed.

"Yes! Yes! That is what I want—a sound mind!"

Why did it seem so difficult?

I wanted a sound mind. I wanted to think clearly. I wanted to see my blessings and count them. I wanted to get through a day without crying. I wanted to dance in the kitchen and go to the store without feeling like a failure. I could not seem to do anything well enough. All the confidence and calmness that I once had quickly vanished.

My soundness had been snatched away without warning. I was paralyzed in my own crazy, but I did not know how I got there or how to escape. So I sobbed. Today will be another day like the rest. I will do my best. I will try hard. I will feed my kids. I will be a good mom. I will be a good wife. I will be a good pastor's wife. I will try to fulfill my many responsibilities, and maybe if I succeed, I will feel better tomorrow.

I tried and I tried. Something was constantly lacking. I could not seem to get it right. If I did succeed, I would eventually end up in the same place, with tears, confusion, and failure. I knew

I should be reading my Bible, so I did. I would stare at the pages and wonder why I was not getting a miraculous word. I needed help, and I was seeking it. I felt trapped, but there was no escape. I think we all have these moments in life when we wonder why we aren't experiencing God's deliverance like we want to.

If you are feeling trapped, it is time to examine your perspective. Just like my little boy looks at a bruised banana and sees its potential, I look at the bruises of life and see the possibilities of God's sovereignty. We may never fully grasp all that God is doing in the crazy seasons of life that we go through, but I have learned and am learning that there truly is a reason for every season.

No Exaggerating

As I stood in the kitchen that day, my mind was filled with the chaos of life. It's as if the scrambled eggs spoke confusion to me. The fogginess of my brain made me feel weepy, alone, and like I was the only person alive who had ever felt such turmoil. When I take a step back and look at the reality of life, I can see clearly now. I can understand that I was a tired, run-down mom who truly needed more sleep. My view of life was deformed. Everything bad that happened seemed huge. It was as if I deemed each

> *The bad things in life are many and will always take a front seat if we allow them to.*

day terrible after one little spill or mistake. I wish I could go back to that season and view life through a clear lens. I would give that worn-out mama a word of encouragement. "You don't have to measure up. God loves you even though you haven't showered for four days. Your children will grow up super fast, so hold them, rock them, and look deep into their eyes as many times a day as you can. But most of all, tell them all about Jesus. You're a good mom."

No Badge of Courage

Big things happen in life, some good and some terrible. It is easy to allow the bad things to take center stage in our minds, hearts, and conversations. Just think of when someone asks you how your week is going. If life is good, there's really not much to talk about. I mean, the kids are healthy, the husband is loving, the job is paying well, and food is on the table. But when the money is tight and the doctor report is devastating, these are the things that fill our conversations. If we don't have our own tragedy, we talk about other people's problems. For some reason we feel justified in our gossip if we are sharing something that needs prayer. We don't necessarily pray over it for an hour, but we yak about it on the phone for an hour and don't think twice. The bad things in life are many and will always take a front seat if we allow them to.

I love how Francis Chan addresses our view of problems in his book *Crazy Love*. He says, "When I am consumed by my problems—stressed out about my life, my family, my job—I actually convey the belief that I think the circumstances are more important than God's command to always rejoice. In other words, that I have the 'right' to disobey God because of the magnitude of my responsibilities."[1]

I am ashamed to say I have allowed my troubles and trials to take the front seat many times and drive my life for weeks, months, and even years. If you are dealing with tough issues, it's natural for it to make your stomach hurt, make your head pound, and be the center of what you talk about and think about. It's much harder to pray about it. I know. I have worn my problems as a badge on my shoulder many more times than I would like to confess. What if we unpinned the badge and placed it in God's hands? We would be free from carrying that heavy weight. No, our circumstances would not change, but our conversation could. Instead of looking at the badge every day, all day, we could place it in Jesus' hands and look at Him all day, every day. That's how we live with an anchored perspective.

Accept Your Struggle

Earlier in the book, I mentioned my biological dad. It took many years for me to accept the fact that he left me behind. I fought with God for years over the reality of the situation. I looked at it through shaded glasses, thinking there must be a really good reason why a daddy would leave his daughter. When I finally came to grips with the facts, I was able to process the past and move forward. I did not get over and forget everything that ever happened, but my focus shifted from what my dad did to me to what God can do through me. You see, God has used my story in many lives to help others with similar problems. When I realized that God could use me to encourage others to forgive, heal, and move forward, my focus was shifted from me to He. If God is the center of my life, it will not matter what happens to me. What will matter is how I view myself and my life. If I view myself as a victim, I will continually feel victimized. If I view myself as God's child, I will continually feel victorious. God has helped me change my perspective. God can help you too.

Assume Your Position

God has a purpose for your life that was established before the foundation of the world. Just as the banana starts out new, protected, and unharmed, your life began as a tiny miracle perfectly designed by God. As you've grown, you have been different places and traveled different paths. There may be places you hope to never return to, and there may be scars that you have received along the way. Some of us have been tenderly cared for and bear fewer marks. But some are deeply scarred and carry big, unimaginable wounds. It may seem like you will never be complete or whole, but God promises to make all things new. He is the answer that we all desperately long for.

Remember the children playing in the ocean in the last chapter? They had no idea about the possibilities of danger that lurked. They could not see the dangerous sea creatures or the rip tides beneath the surface. Some children's eyes are opened early to the wounds that life can produce. Their little lives might be marred in the early years of their life. God is teaching me that no matter what we go through or how difficult it may be, His arms are always waiting, and His Word is always there. God wants you and me to see Him. He wants His children to assume their position as His. When we put our faith in Jesus as our Savior, we have a purpose to fulfill. It is not to escape the hard times, to exaggerate life, or to wear a badge of honor displaying all we have been through. Our purpose is to love God and give Him glory. When we do, no matter how bruised and battered we are from the life we have endured, His sweet fruit will be produced in our lives.

View Life with Purpose

When God peels back the layers of pain and heartache and the strength of His grace and mercy is revealed in our lives, it is beautiful. There is nothing like the fruit of God's amazing grace. I have seen it with my eyes. I have experienced it in my own life. God's fruit is priceless.

Sometimes I feel like a bruised banana, and it seems as if I do not have much to offer. But God sees the fruit. In fact, God produces the fruit. I do not have to try to produce what I cannot create. God creates all things. He gives life. He saves souls. He lifts burdens, and He calms waters. When life is overwhelming and it seems like you might sink to the bottom of the ocean, God is with you through it all. He transforms burdens in your life to blessings.

I know it is not easy to see beyond the trials of life. They often take center stage and parade in all their glory, whether it's failure, fear, or frustration. This is the enemy trying to compromise your perspective. If he can get you to focus on your problems rather than on God, the enemy is accomplishing his goal. Remember: the devil wants to destroy, and he won't stop when you feel like you are going to collapse. The enemy wants you to continue to feel the pain of the wounds you have experienced over and over again. But Jesus has a greater purpose, plan, and providence for each of us. When we begin to see beyond the bruises of life into the eternal kingdom of God, our lives take on a new purpose. No longer do we live actively defeated by what we have done or what has happened to us, but we live actively in pursuit of God's presence and power. When we hand over the hard parts of life to God's control, we live in expectation of seeing His fruit. The fruit of God's power is rarely an easy life, but it's always a beautiful one—one that exchanges the bruises for blessings.

> To all who mourn in Israel, he will give a crown of beauty
> for ashes, a joyous blessing instead of mourning, festive
> praise instead of despair. In their righteousness, they will
> be like great oaks that the LORD has planted for his own
> glory. (Isaiah 61:3 NLT)

When we change our perspective of the bruises of life, knowing there is an eternal purpose, we learn the power of

God's presence in our greatest pain. I would never wish hard times on anyone, but I'm learning that God, in all His glory, shows up in the midst of every problem I face. And for that, I am willing to walk through the problems of this world in order to learn more about how strong His power really is.

Questions to Ponder

1. List some of the bruises and scars from your past.

2. In what ways has God used those scars for His purpose?

3. What burden have you worn as a badge of honor?

4. How can you hand that burden over to God for His glory?

5. What experiences of your past could become fruit for your future and for others?

Praying God's Power

Dear Heavenly Father,

I never could have anticipated all that my life would hold. If I knew then what I know now, I would have done things differently. Sometimes my heart hurts when I think back on what I have endured. I don't want to carry my burdens like a badge, and I don't want my problems to form my perspective. I want to be open to Your will and to produce sweet fruit. I want to see beyond myself, and I want to help others gain victorious ground. I know that in order to see fruit I must walk with You and allow You to guide me, lead me, and teach me. As I walk forward today, please show me exactly how to release my burdens and my badge. I don't want to hold on to it anymore. I want to be free to see fruit.

In Jesus' name, amen.

Experiencing God's Presence

Incline Your ear, O LORD, and answer me;
For I am afflicted and needy.
Preserve my soul, for I am a godly man;
O You my God, save Your servant who trusts in
    You.
Be gracious to me, O Lord,
For to You I cry all day long.
Make glad the soul of Your servant,
For to You, O Lord, I lift up my soul.
For You, Lord, are good, and ready to forgive,
And abundant in lovingkindness to all who call
    upon You.
Give ear, O LORD, to my prayer;
And give heed to the voice of my supplications!
In the day of my trouble I shall call upon You,
For You will answer me.

—Psalm 86:1-7 (NASB)

Part 4

Anchored in the Promise of God's Presence

Three Steps to Experiencing God's Power

Chapter 10

Step 1: Listen to His Voice

Surely I have calmed and quieted my soul,
Like a weaned child with his mother;
Like a weaned child is my soul within me.
—Psalm 131:2 (NKJV)

Childlike Faith

One night, I tucked my sweet boy into his bed; we said our prayers, talked about the day, and read one of his favorite books. When I leaned in to give him a kiss, his words compelled me to listen to the depth of his heart. In a sweet whisper and toddler tone he said, "God speaks quiet to us." Without a thought I answered, "What does He say?" His innocent face looked up and waited. With precious little answers about things we prayed about, he repeated his pattern of looking up, listening, and relaying the answer that he was waiting to hear from God. We repeated this process three times. I asked him a final time if God said anything else. He listened again. With his sparkling blue eyes looking into mine and the innocent, sincere smile of a child, my son said, "He loves us."

For days after, I could not stop replaying my little boy's words in my mind. "God speaks quiet to us." "He loves us." It rang over and over in my head. If only I would stop and listen more, then I could hear God more. If only I could turn down the noise of life, then I could hear God calling me more. I long to hear His voice. As my child looked up into heaven that night, I wonder what he saw and what God's voice sounded like to him. I was a little bit (OK, a lot) disappointed that I hadn't heard the same thing. But then again, had I really slowed down to listen?

Sometimes when we are really longing for God's power in our lives, we think we need a burning bush moment or a miracle of water turning into wine to truly see all the glory and power of His presence. It seems at times that God is giving us the silent treatment rather than the miracle we imagine we need. I'm learning the power I desire from God is in the quiet, still moments where nothing is competing with God's voice. It is in those moments that I experience His manifest presence in my life.

God used the words of my little boy to speak to me. God told me to slow down, turn my eyes to Him, and listen. It's not that God was giving me the silent treatment, but sometimes He speaks quietly to me, and other times He just wants me to remember that He loves me. When I stop, look to God, and listen, I hear Him. Sometimes rather than looking for writing in the sky or laying out a fleece in a rainstorm, we just need to quiet our souls and listen.

And he said, Go forth, and stand upon the mount before the LORD. And, behold, the LORD passed by, and a great and strong wind rent the mountains, and brake in pieces the rocks before the LORD; but the LORD was not in the wind: and after the wind an earthquake; but the LORD was not in the earthquake: and after the earthquake a fire; but the LORD was not in the fire: and after the fire a still small voice. (1 Kings 19:11-12 KJV)

"A still small voice," Scripture says. That's where He was found. Sometimes we look for God in the big, bombastic circumstances of life. We assume a tragedy or heartbreaking situation is God's way of getting our attention or telling us something we need to fix. What if that tragedy or the struggle your family faces is just the result of a broken world?

Sometimes God does use circumstances to speak, but His

> *When we finally learn the value of listening to God, we begin to understand the validity of His voice.*

Word is clear that all tragedies are not God chastising, correcting, or convicting His children. In John 9, Jesus heals a man that was blind from his birth. What a terrible birth defect that would leave a person devastated and seeking answers. But God is clear when the disciples speak up and question Jesus about whose sin caused such a terrible result.

They asked, "Master, who did sin, this man, or his parents, that he was born blind?" (John 9:2 KJV). Jesus corrects them,

"Neither hath this man sinned, nor his parents: but that the works of God should be made manifest in him" (v. 3 KJV).

God shows himself through circumstances good and bad, but we can't assume God is speaking something that He is not. When we are tempted to assume God is saying something, we must quiet our hearts, listen, and interpret God's voice for ourselves, not through the opinions of others. If God is silent, wait. When He speaks, you will know. He speaks, and He speaks often, so if it feels like a pause, continue to press in until you hear Him above any other voice.

The Spirit and the Word of Truth

The Bible is clear that those who believe will hear from God. Yet so many of us continue the struggle to listen to His voice. When we finally learn the value of listening to God, we begin to understand the validity of His voice.

> Therefore Pilate said to Him, "So You are a king?" Jesus answered, "You say correctly that I am a king. For this I have been born, and for this I have come into the world, to testify to the truth. Everyone who is of the truth hears My voice." (John 18:37 NASB)

Before we go any farther, I want to be clear about the voice of God we are listening for. It's not an audible voice or a vision in the night, although I believe God is big enough to do that in our day. But in this generation God speaks to those who believe the truth of His Word and who trust the transforming power of

Jesus. When we choose to accept Jesus into our lives, we receive the gift of hearing from Him through the Holy Spirit. I love the way Priscilla Shirer puts it in her book *Discerning the Voice of God*: "The most spectacular way God has ever spoken to His people is the way He speaks to us right now—through the indwelling, intimate, incredible gift of His Spirit and the timeless, living, holy Word of God."[1]

God Loves You

When God seems silent, it can feel like His favor is wavering and the anchor that once held us securely seems to have drifted away. When my husband lay in a hospital bed for days on end, or when my biological dad didn't call on my birthday for the fifteenth year in a row, I felt discouragement deep in my soul. When we desperately want to hear from God but His voice seems lost somewhere between our desperate pleas and the clouds that linger overhead, it's vital to remember that God loves us. There are times we truly don't know how to hear God's voice. If we could remember the simple facts that God loves us and wants to speak to us, we would be so free to walk through the troubles of life without the agony of wondering if God truly cares about us, hears us, and wants to answer us. Living an anchored life doesn't mean life is easy and that God is going to fix every problem perfectly, answer every question audibly, and come through with a miracle and confetti falling from the sky, but it does mean we can learn to live in a posture of expectancy. When we begin to expect God's reply because of the simple fact that we know He cares, we will remember how strong of an anchor He really is. God's love goes beyond anything we can fathom and yet over and over again we doubt because we can't see, hear, or touch him.

Do you ever feel that you just want a glimpse of Him? I mean, if you could just see Him for one second or talk face-to-face, then you would really know. But then the Holy Spirit speaks to you, and you think, *Oh, right. You were there all along. I just didn't trust You.*

I think we all know that God is present and listens to our desires (even on the days that our desires aren't His), but when we get wrapped up in the hard times of life, we begin to feel as if God is far away. Trouble surrounds us, and we feel alone, afraid, and discouraged. We know what God's Word says about the Holy Spirit being the comforter and our helper, but sometimes it feels like we need more power from the Holy One. Then we would feel anchored, secure.

When we begin to realize where to focus our listening skills—on the Spirit and the Word—we are well on our way to hearing His voice. The Word is the external source of power, and the Spirit is the internal interpreter of the Word that ignites God's power. These two together are an irreplaceable pair. The Word provides wisdom while the Spirit interprets the Scripture and gives each believer the specific word he or she needs to hear from God. The Word speaks truth to us while the Spirit is truth living inside us. When we realize we possess this power within our own souls, it should compel us to want to hear more truth and less of the information of the world.

When we allow the world to fill us on the inside, we can expect the woes of the world to flow from us on the outside, and it's not a pretty sight. When we allow truth to fill us on the inside, we can expect God's power to flow from us on the outside. And who doesn't want that to be how friends and family see us? It's how we want to live, isn't it? I think if we can capture this, we will crave more and more of Him and His words to us through His active voice. But sometimes we question if we are hearing Him.

Listening Skills

Have you ever thought, *I must not be hearing God correctly*? I know I have thought that a time or two (or more). We often want to hear from God the way *we* want to hear from God, and sometimes it affects the way we listen to Him.

There are no right words to say, correct position for, or secret pathway to the Holy Spirit's presence. The Bible is clear that if we seek, we will find. Why do we struggle so much to feel like we have found Him? I think one of the biggest barriers between a Christian woman and her access to feeling the Holy Spirit's presence is the ability and vulnerability of her listening skills.

Believing positions us perfectly for receiving. That's the art of listening.

God often speaks into the quiet places of a burdened heart. If our hearts are so filled with trouble and we hold tightly to the problems that we are experiencing, we will have a very difficult time allowing the Holy Spirit to dominate our hearts' motives, desires, and actions. If we cannot listen, we will never hear. Listening to God requires a posture of prayer—not a physical posture, but a spiritual one. It requires a heart, mind, and life fully surrendered to the holy God of heaven knowing He knows more than we do. We must submit as a sheep surrenders to a shepherd. Sheep listen for their master's voice and follow where he leads them—without going on their own path.

> "My sheep hear my voice, and I know them, and they
> follow me." (John 10:27)

Other translations say, "My sheep listen to My voice." I love to think that if I am God's child (sheep), I will hear Him. But we must understand the reality that only those who listen will truly hear. The sheep that don't listen don't stay close to Him and ultimately don't hear Him.

When we refuse to listen and we go our own way, we suffer in silence. We will never completely hear and understand what He really has to say to us until we get close, stay close, and desire what He desires. He wants our hearts and our holiness, nothing else.

Sometimes when we don't listen, we eventually learn the hard way what God was speaking to us when we refused to listen. And we see how much we missed out on: experiencing His leading, His comfort, His peace, His calmness, His conviction, His guidance, His love, and most of all, His power.

When we choose to listen, we are proving we believe in

God's power. Believing positions us perfectly for receiving. That's the art of listening.

> My son, if you will receive my words
> And treasure my commandments within you,
> Make your ear attentive to wisdom,
> Incline your heart to understanding;
> For if you cry for discernment,
> Lift your voice for understanding;
> If you seek her as silver
> And search for her as for hidden treasures;
> Then you will discern the fear of the LORD
> And discover the knowledge of God.
> For the LORD gives wisdom;
> From His mouth come knowledge and under-
> standing.
>
> —Proverbs 2:1-6 (NASB)

When we receive God's words, which I take to mean "to pay attention to and accept," we begin to "discover the knowledge of God." We can see that God speaks and that He gives us His wisdom for every circumstance in life. As we "make our ear attentive" to God, we begin to hear more and more. And in an age where knowledge is keen, don't we want to hear what God has to say to us? If we are to live anchored to Him, it's essential that we not only believe we will hear Him but also receive His words when they come.

Turn Down the Distractions

The phone rang, and I saw the name of my dear friend. I knew I did not have much time, but I thought I could listen to her talk while I did the dishes, laundry, and other chores I needed to finish up around the house. I picked up the phone and began the conversation. At every silent pause, I would say, "Uh-huh." We continued for at least an hour as I hustled around getting everything done that I needed to while I tried to balance the phone pressed between my ear and my shoulder. When she began to run out of things to talk about, she said, "Well, I guess I'll talk to you later," and we hung up the phone. As I thought about our conversation later, I could not remember what she talked about during my hour of hustling around. Shame filled my heart. I knew something important kept us on the phone for over an hour, but in the midst of my busyness to do what I thought was most important, I chose chores over listening to my friend.

We often do the same thing to God. We rush around doing what we think is important, and we miss the words that God is trying to speak into our hearts. We want to hear Him, but life simply gets in the way, and we miss Him. Sometimes we start out with big, bold plans of doing something amazing for God only to get swept up in the details, the stress of the daily grind, and the distractions of the to-do list that is seemingly required to get the job done. Oh, how foolish we can be when it comes to what is most important. We often choose the current over the eternal. And when we do, often we later see how our choice to focus on what felt crucial was really a distraction from what God was trying to draw us to—Himself.

Listen

Our world is filled with so much noise it's often difficult to stay focused and listen to God. The constant flow of the newsfeeds and notifications take so much time and mental and emotional energy from us each day that it's hard to truly shut out the distractions. We stand with our phones in our hands or pockets, making everyone and everything that enters our world compete with it. Some days I'm left holding the phone between my shoulder and my ear, saying, "Uh-huh," thinking I'll hear everything I need to hear from God and really be able to understand His voice amid the noise of unlimited information. The truth is we will never pick out His voice until we put away the distractions and set aside designated time and get to be alone with God. The Holy Spirit's power is freely offered for all who seek Him, but too often we are busy seeking our own answers and our own agendas for a new, faster way to do life in general. Trolling Pinterest or other sites takes precedence over our listening skills, and everything we want to hear from God is drowned out by the information flooding through our electronic devices all day long.

It might seem impossible to get away and truly hear from God every day. We start thinking we might miss something if we take time away from the constant connection for a while. On top of that, the rat race of life has us running full steam ahead, and there is literally not enough time in a day to do it all. By the time we finally get to bed each night, we whisper a prayer and, before we can say amen, drift off to sleep. When the alarm clock goes off and the day begins, it's a dash to the finish line. Breakfast, showers, backpacks, lunches, outfits, school, work, chores, dinner, a favorite show in the evening. If there's any time left, maybe we'll read a good book; and if there's any energy left after that, we squeeze in time with our husbands or load the dishwasher so we won't see dirty dishes in the morning. We truly don't know when to find time for God.

I get it. I'm in the hustle and bustle too. I rush out the door, cook, clean, and wipe faces every day. I sweep a hundred times a week and watch the empty laundry basket overflow in one day, then crawl into bed with a man who needs me. It's exhausting. But the key is in acknowledging God every moment of your day, listening for what He has specifically for you. When the alarm goes off, thank God and ask Him how to use your time wisely. When breakfast is being prepared, thank Him for hands that work and food that fills hungry bellies. When you sit down to eat, admire God's provision. When you dress a child, thank Him for life. When a child speaks, listen to the innocence and look into the eyes that don't yet know how much evil fills this world. When your husband pulls you close, let your heart be mesmerized by the beauty of love. When work feels overwhelming, praise God for the gifts and talents He's given you. When the house looks like a tornado came through, tell God, "Thank You for a home." And in every moment you breathe, listen. He's speaking in the mundane moments of your day. Through children's giggles and smiles, He tells me, "You're a good mama; keep it up. Your work is not in vain." Through a tight embrace by my husband, He says, "You are fearfully and wonderfully made. You are a woman with a high calling." Through the slobbery kisses of a toddler, He says, "Motherhood is a full-time job, but it won't last forever." Through Kool-Aid stains on the carpet, He says, "Life is more important than spills. Don't sweat the small stuff. I'm much more important." Through the touch of an elderly lady in the community, He says, "Be faithful, and cherish every moment of life." Through people all around us, He encourages our hearts by a kind word, a thoughtful deed, or a generous gift of the exact amount we need on the precise date we need it. God is speaking to us in so many different ways each day; it's up to us to listen.

Through the Bible, God convicts my heart and gives me grace and time to change. Through my posture of prayer every day, He never ceases to speak. God speaks through the big and small moments of the day when we listen. God's voice fills me with His power when I choose to be in His presence.

Hearing from God is not reserved for a chosen few. Hearing God's voice is a priceless gift that we get to experience every single day *if* we listen. When Jesus left the earth to live with His Father in heaven, He left the Holy Spirit to dwell within us.

His words leave us speechless when we think about the power they offer:

> And I will pray the Father, and He will give you another
> Helper, that He may abide with you forever—the Spirit of

truth, whom the world cannot receive, because it neither
sees Him nor knows Him; but you know Him, for He
dwells with you and will be in you. (John 14:16-17 NKJV)

That helper is the Holy Spirit. The Amplified version describes the Holy Spirit as a comforter, counselor, helper, inter-
cessor, advocate, strengthener, and standby. Do you love all the
roles the Holy Spirit plays in our lives? It makes me feel secure
and confident to know that the Spirit is all of these things to us.

If we look back in Samuel's day, the Bible says:

The word of the LORD was rare in those days; there was no
widespread revelation. (1 Samuel 3:1b NKJV)

Today, we have the Holy Spirit of God dwelling inside us,
and yet we still wrestle and struggle and fight and wonder,
Where is God? The problem is not that God's voice is rare or
that the Holy Spirit is reserving His power for a chosen, perfect
disciple. The problem is that we, in our own self-absorbed
thinking, do not listen long enough to hear from God. If we
would quiet our souls, lives, minds, hearts, and homes, we could
learn the art of listening in a way that we haven't experienced
before. Sometimes this means taking drastic action, like getting
away to rest, retreat, and allow God's voice to speak into the
silence of solitude. It might mean kneeling at an altar of a
church, or beside the bed, pressing your knees to the carpet
and humbling yourself physically as you confess the struggle
you have with listening. Sometimes without even realizing it,
we distance ourselves from God because of the noise we allow

to fill up our lives. When we listen for God's voice only when we want something, we are missing the value of His voice.

When we discipline ourselves to listen to Him daily, giving Him our first thoughts and undivided attention, we begin to learn the value of turning down the volume of life and tuning in to the sound of God's voice.

> *It is not about what I say to God through my prayers; it is what God says to me.*

Sometimes He doesn't speak as soon as we submit. This is when we must not quit. God's voice will speak to a surrendered heart. Linger a little longer, and ask God to make Himself known to you. It might mean teaching your children to sit quietly and read or creating a place in the home where you get alone with God. The key is quieting the distractions that compete for our constant attention so our minds and hearts have nothing else to consider. He will speak as much and as long as we listen.

We need to learn to live in a posture of prayer continually. We need to listen and look attentively for God in as many moments of our day as we can. We will see Him in the eyes of the lady at the checkout. We will notice Him in the words of a child's sincere "I love you." We will hear God ask, "Is that really best?" when we want to snap back with a good comeback to someone. We will understand what real love is when our hearts feel the nudge to give. It is not about what I say to God through my prayers; it is what God says to me. As soon as we ignore our posture of prayer throughout the day and stop listening to His voice, we forfeit His power in our lives.

What if we come to realize we need God every single moment of every single day? Can you imagine how differently we would live if we were completely in tune with God all day, every day? No longer would anxiety hit our stomachs and make our heads pound. The still, small voice of God would linger like a safe haven over our heads, and we would know we have no reason to fear. When a difficult situation arises, our faith would carry us because we would hear the words God says louder than we hear the words of this world. God's power is able to sustain us like that. What if for one day, every time something went wrong, we immediately prayed and expected God to act on our behalf? I don't mean we thought about praying. I mean we actually called on the One who we believe has the power to help us in every situation and anticipated that He would respond to us. Power is found in Him when we pray and when we listen.

Experiencing the Holy Spirit

Have you ever begged God to work something out a certain way only for Him to work it out in an entirely different way? When I watched my husband struggle for strength in the hospital bed, I begged God to reveal cancer to us. At least then we could begin treatment, and he could possibly get better. But God knew so much more than I did about the situation. He knew there was no cancer to be found in Rob's body. He also knew that the undiagnosed illness that was killing Rob would be over soon and he would get better. Too many times we do what we think is right by telling God what we need Him to do. We tell Him exactly what we need and how we want things to work out. And then we walk away thinking, *I sure did a good job praying today.*

Rather than telling God how to fix our problems, what if we just went to His feet and listened to what He had to say? The key is to watch our words, shut off the thoughts of *What about this?* and *How about that?* and say like Samuel, "Speak, LORD, for your servant hears" (1 Samuel 3:9 NKJV). In the hospital with my husband, I would have saved myself so much agony if I would have just listened to God's voice as we wrestled with Rob's illness.

I love how Francis Chan puts it in his book *Crazy Love*: "What if I said, 'Stop praying'? What if I told you to stop talking *at* God for a while, but instead to take a long, hard look at Him before you speak another word? Solomon warned us not to rush into God's presence with words. That's what fools do. And often, that's what we do."[2]

Listening does not usually come naturally for us. As we take steps toward becoming aware of the Holy Spirit's presence, let's position ourselves to listen. I am amazed how God speaks so clearly to me when I simply shut everything down, put the phone away, get alone, and listen. He gives hope when we ask for help. He gives peace when we seek Him instead of our own source of pleasure. And He speaks into a listening heart when we are willing to learn from those more experienced than us.

Hearing from God is not a mystical practice or a meditative

meeting but a realization that God truly cares for you right where you are. I would encourage you to put away everything that normally captivates your attention and ask God to make Himself real to you. Think of your listening relationship with God as something that needs growth. Nothing ever starts full-grown. Usually life springs from a tiny seed, and it needs some type of outside source of nurture to feed it. In this case your listening skills need solitude, silence, a Bible, and a willing heart ready and eager to hear from God. I think one of the best places to start in your Bible to identify with those who also wanted to hear from God is Psalms or Proverbs. David's cry to know God is so compelling for us to know and hear today. And the kings who wrote Proverbs, including Solomon, shared wisdom from God that we can apply every single day.

If you are listening to the voice of God daily or on a regular basis, the trials that normally take your breath away will be navigated by God's all-knowing, all-powerful peace and comfort. It does not mean that you won't be disappointed or even completely brokenhearted. It means God will carry you through the trial. His power will overwhelm you as you listen to His voice of care and correction.

As we walk through things that hurt us deeply within our chests and literally make our hearts ache, we can feel relief in knowing that within the same chest lives a comforter, a healer, and a helper who knows every single detail of our lives. We can feel His power over the worst problems we've ever experienced, and we can learn to live anchored even when it seems as if life is drowning us and drenching us in heartache.

When you feel like the problem is too big and the storm will never end, He will give you exactly what you need when you need it. If you are far away from Him and run to Him during the storm, He will be there. And how comforting it is to feel Him near the moment you get the phone call or bad report.

I sat in the car and breathed deeply, trying to let my head understand what my heart was feeling. I realized the difficulty of the road my dad would be facing with cancer, and I cried. But deep within, I knew God would carry us every step of the way, no matter what the steps looked like. That's my anchor. It's choosing to listen to the still, small voice inside that says, "I'm with you," even when the world is saying everything is falling apart. If you are anchored in His power and presence continually, you will not be swept away or taken under at every wave that threatens your life.

God's presence is like nothing man can offer. God may use man to encourage, uplift, and help, but true power is found in bowing at Jesus' feet and listening to His voice day by day. As God's child, you have access to that power. You don't need to wrestle and struggle and fret about the future. You can live in God's power every day when you live expecting to hear from Him.

If you only remember one thing from this chapter, take the advice of a four-year-old little boy who seemed to grasp the concept of listening to God: "God speaks quiet to us. He loves us." And listen.

Questions to Ponder

1. How can you be a better listener?

2. What in your life is keeping you from hearing from God?

3. Recall a specific time you experienced God's voice through a person, an event, or His Word.

4. What need do you have in your life where you expect God to speak to you?

5. How did God speak to you through this chapter?

Praying God's Power

Dear Heavenly Father,

I desperately want to hear from You. I want You to surround me and carry me through the life I live. You know every detail of my life. You have seen me when I yearn for You and when I don't listen to Your voice at all. I want to rest in Your presence. I want to sit at Your feet. I want to hear Your voice and sense Your power. I need You to make Yourself real to me today. I need to hear from You. I quiet my soul and listen. I choose right now to turn off the voices that fight for my attention, and I seek You alone. Please show me Your presence, fill me with power, and let me hear You speak into the silence of this moment.

In Jesus' name, amen.

Experiencing God's Presence

LORD, my heart is not haughty,
Nor my eyes lofty.
Neither do I concern myself with great matters,
Nor with things too profound for me.
Surely I have calmed and quieted my soul,
Like a weaned child with his mother;
Like a weaned child is my soul within me.
O Israel, hope in the LORD
From this time forth and forever.

—Psalm 131 (NKJV)

Chapter 11

Step 2: Let God Define the Dream

> For my thoughts are not your thoughts,
>   neither are your ways my ways, declares
>   the LORD.
> For as the heavens are higher than the earth,
>   so are my ways higher than your ways
>   and my thoughts than your thoughts.
>   —Isaiah 55:8-9

My Plans, My Dreams

Opening my crisp, new planner, I perused the empty pages and thought through what the new year would hold. I put my pink pen to the page and began filling in the dates of the events, birthdays, and plans I knew would fill up each month of life. My life was full to the brim, and not much could be added to my agenda. I do this every year. I purchase a beautiful new planner, and I begin dreaming. I think of what the future holds and imagine the goals and dreams I might conquer. I daydream about traveling and accomplishing big things for God.

The past few years of life, God has been working on me in the dream department. Although I want to think I know what God wants for me, I'm learning more and more that God does not always give me the five-year plan like I would prefer. God's dreams instead come one teeny, tiny step at a time, and if I really pay attention, I might get it right the first time around. Many times I jump ahead in my own power and planning and end up having to backpedal to the place God intended all along.

Looking back on some of my planners of the past, I never would have included the things that ended up filling my life. I never dreamed of an emergency wisdom tooth removal or vertigo that would land me in an emergency room, unable to care for my children. I never dreamed of strained relationships, loss, or cancer. But God knows about these things that are going to fill our calendars before they even happen. He knows the things He will call us to when we think we have it all figured out. He knows the people He will put in our path, and He knows who will obey His call and follow through each step of the way.

We're Expecting!

Foster care was never written in my planner. Although I babysat by age eleven, the thought of caring for someone else's children did not interest me in my thirties. Oh, I love babies, but handing them back to their mother's arms after they pooped or spat up filled me with a sense of relief that cannot be explained. I often told my friends I'm not good at taking care of other people's children, as a way to warn them not to ask me to babysit. Perhaps I was trying to coerce myself out of what God was telling me, but I could not wrap my mind around why God would want our family to foster. My patience was thin enough with my own children. Cleaning up spilled milk after my own little pumpkin was bearable, but the thought of cleaning up after more than my own didn't sound exciting or fun and definitely not like a dream come true.

When God made it clear that He was leading my husband and me into foster care, I was baffled and shocked, and I wrestled in my mind with all the reasons why we shouldn't. I tried to talk myself into it and out of it all in the same breath.

As we've already established, when God speaks to His children, He expects obedience. We knew what God had said to us. We knew what we needed to do. I was scared of the unknowns and terrified of the reality and the harsh awareness that I might give seasons of my life away to care for a child that I might not get to keep. I knew I might spend sleepless nights loving, rocking, and singing to a child, and learning a new sort of patience with him or her, only to get a call that the birth parents were ready for their child's return home. A baby I made mine could be ripped from my hands with no time to transition. And then God gently reminded me of Hannah. Her dream and her destiny was not about the baby or a season of self-gratification. It was about God's purpose, God's plan, and God's glory. God had been teaching me these things through His Word, and they began to become real in my life. Suddenly I was forced to live what I believed in my heart or reject the very real voice of God.

> And Samuel grew, and the LORD was with him and let none of his words fall to the ground. And all Israel from Dan to Beersheba knew that Samuel was established as a prophet of the LORD. And the LORD appeared again at Shiloh, for the LORD revealed himself to Samuel at Shiloh by the word of the LORD. (1 Samuel 3:19-21)

No matter how hard it is to understand God's direction in our lives, when He speaks, we must listen and obey His voice and realize He has the master plan. He knows the details and the outcomes before we even choose to follow or reject His leading. We can try to scheme and paste our five-year plan on the wall of our lives for all to see, but God's purpose will always prevail.

We can't manipulate our dreams and call them God's. God's dreams require surrender to His glory alone.

When we think of the story of Hannah and Samuel in the Bible, we often idolize Hannah's heartfelt prayer, lifting her up as the purpose and pearl of the story. But we must remember the purpose of every part of the Bible: God's glory. When God revealed Himself to Samuel, we *could* look back at the story and praise Hannah again. She must have continued praying for her son throughout his life. And I'm sure she did. But God didn't reveal Himself to Samuel so that Hannah could be praised or applauded for her devoted prayer life. And God doesn't speak to us for our own glory either. God didn't let Samuel in on a blessing so Hannah could be lifted up and praised as an accomplished woman or so Samuel could be edified and idolized as someone who had a special revelation from God. God revealed Himself to Samuel so that God's purpose would prevail and God's Word would be spoken to the Israelites through Samuel. It's always about God and His ways. Although God blessed Hannah with a baby, the plan was so much bigger than Hannah could have ever dreamed. Who knew her son would spend his entire life serving God with his whole heart? This is something many of us dream of. To know that our children walk in truth would be a blessing beyond compare. But if we do experience that dream come true, we must remember the purpose—not our glory but God's. Everything—every dream, desire, and desperate plea for deliverance—that is wrapped up in God's power has the potential to transform lives for God's kingdom.

As I faced my fears of becoming a foster mom, God's message to me was clear: "It's My story, Micah, not yours. It's not your season or your struggle or your sacrifice. It's for My glory, for My name's sake, and My purpose. I'm writing a beautiful story of power. You might not see it in the sleepless nights, the early morning feedings, or the loss of a little one you love. But I'm creating something magnificent. Follow Me."

We never know what God will ask of us, but we must remember that He has a dream too! His dream might not involve a white picket fence with two kids and a pool. It might not include the words "stay-at-home mom" or "developing, rising career." God's dreams might take place in the quiet stillness of an embrace of a child in the middle of the night or the cross-country trek of a family who leaves everything they know to tell people they've never met about the God they serve. It could be that God's dream for you includes the words *single, satisfied,* and *secure.* We can't manipulate our dreams and call them God's. God's dreams require surrender to His glory alone. God's dreams are bigger than ours. They change lives, mend broken lives, reveal Jesus in the hardest of places, and ultimately His dreams change the destiny of people in ways we could never manufacture.

> Great is our Lord, and of great power: his understanding is infinite. (Psalm 147:5 KJV)

The Naked Tree

I pulled the ornaments from the tree one by one. I wrapped them carefully and reminisced about the places we had gone, the people we had visited, and the memories we had made. I put each ornament in a big box and sealed it up tightly until the next year, when we would fill the tree again with the magical, sparkly decorations. I stepped back and gazed at the empty tree. No more shine, no more fluff, no more sparkle. Only branches bare of beauty, covered only with its own green needles. And I began to think of our lives. Each year we fill up our lives with sparkly things we love, and we look for soft, fluffy things to do and exciting places to go. We fill our weekends with fun and give our families things to remember. Some of us collect ornaments along the way to fill the tree with next year. And then one by one, we think on each thing life held. But this year was different for me. God challenged me as I looked at the naked tree.

He challenged me to strip away the sparkles, the fluff, and the desires of my own heart and stand exposed before Him. Not in a physically naked form, although there is no shame before Him, but in a spiritual form. He challenged me to let go of all the stuff that makes my life look good and be willing to come before Him just as I am. As I began to strip away the pretty plans, the nice clothes, the clean home, the sparkly jewels, the makeup, the hair, the children dressed in matching outfits, the family picture where everyone is smiling, the Facebook highlight reel, and all the things that make me look like I have a life of success, I realized I am living a dream come true. Even without all of those things in my life, I have found something that empowers me and gives me worth and purpose in my exposed, naked form. I have found the presence of God, and He has found me.

> *Dreams, real dreams, don't come true without the power and presence of God.*

When we dream for something more than God Himself, we begin to idolize the things in our lives that give us sparkle and shine. We try filling our tree with everything we like, yet when we step back and gaze on it, we wonder why we aren't satisfied. We keep searching for a dream and grasping for something we will never attain.

When we finally begin to strip away all the pretty things and get down to the foundation of who we are, we will see the beauty of God's magnificent creation. There might be missing branches or a few bumps and bruises from the journey, but the bare tree, willing to be seen by the one who created it, is beautiful. This is where I find power in my dreams; I dream of being with God alone.

One day when the earth fades away and we stand before the throne of God, we will all be exposed in a new light. There won't be shiny ornaments to hide the holes in our hearts. There won't be velvet ribbon to contain the wayward branches. There won't be an angel of light topping off our lives, making everything bright. There will be a naked vessel clothed only in the spiritual robe of the dream we chased. Is it Jesus? Is He the one we are after? Is it His purpose that filled our hearts, our minds, and our lives, or is it something else?

> And I saw no temple in the city, for its temple is the Lord
> God the Almighty and the Lamb. And the city has no need
> of sun or moon to shine on it, for the glory of God gives it
> light, and its lamp is the Lamb. By its light will the nations
> walk, and the kings of the earth will bring their glory into
> it, and its gates will never be shut by day—and there will
> be no night there. They will bring into it the glory and the
> honor of the nations. But nothing unclean will ever enter
> it, nor anyone who does what is detestable or false, but
> only those who are written in the Lamb's book of life.
>
> (Revelation 21:22-27)

If you know Jesus, your name is written in the Lamb's book of life. It's time to let Him define your dreams. Say no to the fluff and the sparkles, and say yes to the power of God. The glitter and glam of this world will look dull in heaven. The streets of gold and the mansions being prepared for us are beyond our comprehension. The worldly dreams we seek are so short-sighted and empty. Let's look beyond this moment and time. Let's dream of the eternal impact of our lives in a world where problems take the place of power.

> But seek first the kingdom of God and his righteousness,
> and all these things will be added to you. (Matthew 6:33)

We can make our goals and our lists of dream jobs, dream destinations, dream homes, and dreams of financial freedom, but no matter how much we plan and scheme and manipulate our destiny, we must be ready when God calls us to something that was never in our plans. After birthing our three biological children, we had a plan. But God's plans were different. I don't know how many foster children will walk through our home, but I do know this: God has a dream for them too, an eternal dream. I never imagined I would be a part of that kind of dream. My dreams involved a simple life. My husband, Hannah, Madalyn, Jaxon, and me. Oh, and we would be healthy, and I would see my birth father in heaven, where it would not hurt anymore. But God isn't simple. God is the Savior. A Savior so complex that He sees and knows the detailed dreams of each of our lives and calls us beyond those dreams to a new destiny.

I'm sure you have dreams of your own. Some you've

tucked away for fear they will never be fulfilled, and some you hold tightly in hopes of one day fulfilling the ambitions of your heart. Dreams, real dreams, don't come true without the power and presence of God. Oh, we can manipulate success, save money, and produce results until we feel happy with the outcome, but it will never satisfy if God isn't the author of it. The only satisfaction we will ever find is when we decide to release every dream we've ever dreamed and let God design the direction and destination of our lives.

> His divine power has granted to us all things that pertain to life and godliness, through the knowledge of him who called us to his own glory and excellence, by which he has granted to us his precious and very great promises, so that through them you may become partakers of the divine nature, having escaped from the corruption that is in the world because of sinful desire. (2 Peter 1:3-4)

At the turn of the new year, when we make lists and write down what we want to accomplish, some invest hundreds or even thousands of dollars in planning their best life. They take classes and attend seminars on making their lives the best they can be. I'm not against planning, dreaming, or setting goals, but I'm learning to reshape the way I plan and dream. I'm learning that rather than make my list of goals and dreams in my power and my planner, I must take my notebook or the computer and open it wide, asking God to define my dreams before I put one mark on the page. Just like the naked tree, I must empty myself, my life, and my thoughts and let God do the planning.

God's plans might not include a promotion at work, but it might include a promise of peace in spite of physical success. God's plans might not include a *New York Times* best seller, but it might include a transformation of heart and life as you learn to seek Him with all of your might. God's plans might not include a child, but it might include the birth of a new life in Christ and the power that supersedes your deepest desires of satisfaction. God's plans might not include a knight in shining armor to share a future with, but it might include God's power shining so brightly within you that there's no denying His presence. God's plans might not include the picture-perfect Christmas card or the financial stability you've worked your entire life for, but it might include learning the truth of living anchored in God's power in spite of your biggest disappointments and regrets. God's dreams cannot be defined by the world we live in.

Anytime we see dreams in the Bible, it's in a literal form of an actual dream, a stark difference from the dreams we tend to speak of. The dreams in the Bible had purpose, meaning, and often a message from God Himself. Our dreams hold the same. Those things you long for, plan for, and desperately desire have purpose and meaning and contain a message from God. It's up to us to grab hold of it and embrace it. I don't know God's dream for you, but I do know this: God has a purpose, meaning, and message for you! His purpose is to know Him and give Him glory. His meaning is to love Him and let Him love you. His message is to share Him with others so they can know Him too. We experience power in our dreams when we realize the life we live has the potential to bring others into the eternal kingdom of God.

What is God's dream for you?

> You can make many plans, but the LORD's purpose will
> prevail. (Proverbs 19:21 NLT)

Questions to Ponder

1. Name one dream you have had since your childhood.

2. What is the biggest dream you've ever had?

3. Is there a dream God is asking you to surrender to His control?

4. Has God given you a dream you never knew you wanted before?

5. Are you willing to let God define your dreams even if it means doing something you never imagined or wanted before?

6. Who in your life needs to know about God's eternal kingdom?

Praying God's Power

Dear Heavenly Father,

As I learn more about Your power, I'm beginning to see that Your ways are so much higher than mine. The purpose of my life is not about what I will do or achieve, but it's all about what You will do in me. As I seek to fulfill the dreams in my heart, I pray You will fill me with dreams I never knew were there. Give me wisdom to see Your will and way for my life. I surrender my dreams, desires, and destiny to Your control. From the depths of my heart, I'm asking You to define my dreams.

In Jesus' name, amen.

Experiencing God's Presence

May God be gracious to us and bless us
    and make his face to shine upon us,   *Selah*
that your way may be known on earth,
    your saving power among all nations.
Let the peoples praise you, O God;
    let all the peoples praise you!

Let the nations be glad and sing for joy,
    for you judge the peoples with equity
    and guide the nations upon earth.   *Selah*
Let the peoples praise you, O God;
    let all the peoples praise you!

The earth has yielded its increase;
    God, our God, shall bless us.
God shall bless us;
    let all the ends of the earth fear him!

—Psalm 67

Chapter 12

Step 3: Live in Victory

You make known to me the path of life;
   in your presence there is fullness of joy;
   at your right hand are pleasures
   forevermore.
                              —Psalm 16:11

Rain, Rain Go Away

I was not quite an official teenager when I first experienced a malfunctioning umbrella. Two junior high girls, not quite a hundred pounds, each giggled our way through the seventh grade. Friendship is beautiful when you can laugh at yourself and still love each other sincerely. On this day I had never been so thankful for a true-blue friend. Laura and I left the classroom to make a break for the restroom and entered the torrential downpour. Rain was coming down so heavy that I wanted to turn back. But we began to make our way, giggling down the sidewalk. The laughter escalated so much that we paused in the rain (holding in our full bladders), wishing it would let up. We let the laughter out and hoped to keep the pee in.

We contained ourselves just enough to keep walking, and then, whoosh! Our umbrella gave way to rain collapsing on two awkward, giggling girls. So there we stood, rain running down our backs and faces, and something else running down our legs. Accidents are embarrassing anyway you slice it, but in the seventh grade, you might as well have dug me a grave and put me under.

I had a similar experience in college. Now older and wiser and perhaps a bit more in control of the bladder situation, I was still no match for the rain. My umbrella, although cute as it could be, didn't stand a chance against Florida's sideways rain. The huge raindrops pelted my legs and then my side. And then I felt it on my face. I turned my umbrella, thinking I could block the wind and the rain, but as soon as I did it would change direction. Spinning and fighting, I couldn't keep dry. And then, whoosh! Just like I had experienced in the seventh grade, my umbrella gave way to the rain, and I stood drenched—only this time I was not giggling. The only option was to run. So I ran with all my might to shelter.

Years later I stood in my garage under the protection of the roof and watched as my children jumped in the puddles and let the rain hit their faces with delight. The joy was incomprehensible. Sometimes when we feel like life is flooding our souls with difficult things, we look around and see people enjoying themselves, jumping in the puddles, and making the most of a life that doesn't seem so great to us.

Life rains. Sometimes it's a light sprinkle, and other times it's a torrential downpour threatening the strength of our

> *Our lives must be empty of our own strength to be filled with His.*

umbrella. We learn to laugh at ourselves, our mishaps, and our misfortunes just as we did when we were younger, but then we grow up. When we've had enough and the sideways rain hits us in the face, we get irritated. Then, *whoosh!* Another blow, and we almost lose our umbrella—and our minds.

No matter how difficult life becomes, God never gives way. His anchor never collapses or even entertains the threats of the downpour. With Him, we can stand in the rain fully exposed, weak, and unable to control anything in our lives and yet somehow have strength. Just when it feels like our umbrella of life might break and everything threatens to give way, that's when we experience God's power. It doesn't necessarily come down like a rescuing force taking away the burdens, pains, and problems that make us feel weak, but it fills us with faith, hope, peace, and patience to get through the current downpour.

Too often we fill our lives with worry, anger, resentment, and unforgiveness. We think as long we are struggling, God must not be with us. But it's in the midst of the deepest struggles that God often displays His power. He does not tremble like a weak umbrella, hoping to hold on until we make it through. He is the rock beneath the ground we walk that will not give way even when everything in life crumbles beneath us. When we look around and see destruction, devastation, emptiness, and heartache, we must look deep inside. If you know God, He is there within you, waiting to fill you with His power.

Our lives must be empty of our own strength to be filled with His. As long I hold on to the protection and peace that I gain in my own ways under my own umbrella, the longer I avoid living in God's power. His power in my life requires a broken umbrella of self. I must let go of everything I think I can do to control my life and keep my eyes on the One who has the power to protect me. Power in our lives never comes from what we do or hold or achieve. Power comes when we surrender to the source of the power in our souls.

Empty

I woke up from a sleepless night, and my problems were still there. My adoptive dad was still fighting a tough battle with cancer, and the burdens of life pressed so heavy on my heart. I'm sure you have had your own mornings when the sun comes up, but life seems to stay down. We all want to rise above and move beyond what weighs us down, but sometimes it's hard, even when we know what to do and how to do it. Trust God, right? Obey His voice? Follow Him? It seems too simple, too trite in the midst of it all.

While I knew the steps to experiencing God's power and living anchored in Him, the heaviness of life once again pressed down on me. I felt crushed beneath a life of broken umbrellas. I begged God, as I always do: "Why is my dad sick?" "Why the perplexing problems?"

Even after we've experienced God time and time again, we often find ourselves back in the same place we started when we first looked up to the sky and questioned God. I think back on those long nights as a little girl when I would cry to God and want to know the answers to my hurts deep inside my heart. Although I didn't hear God speak out loud, I recall His presence with me in those early years. Sometimes it's hard to explain His power, but we know He is with us. Our faith anchors us.

Fits and Fights

Living anchored in God's power isn't about never asking God why. Sometimes we shake our fists and have a hissy fit when things don't go our way. I'm pretty sure I just had one yesterday that could go down in the books as one of the worst fits of all time. Standing in the bathroom and looking up to heaven, I begged God to deliver and heal my loved one.

We each process things differently. When tragedy strikes or burdens pile up, some of us will keep it all in until we can't face it anymore. Some will rant and rave until they feel a sense of relief in the moment. Others will post it on social media for all the world to give them a pity party. Others will bottle it all up and not tell a soul as a way of feeling strong within their own soul. Others will stand shaking insecurely like a junior high girl who hopes no one knows the deep dark secret of her accident, giggling on the outside but oh so insecure on the inside. Empty.

What I am learning through my own perplexing problems is that victory in my life is not found in how my life is going or has gone. Victory is found in God's presence. When I try to process all of the baggage, bad times, and bruises in my own mind and power, I fail, fall, and fumble over every little thing that comes my way. When I learned to begin to see things through the lens of God's power, I began to understand a little more about the providence of God. I must be empty so He can fill me. I must be willing so He can use me. I must be humble and know He is holy. I must surrender and let Him be the Savior. This is when I begin to learn what living in victory really means.

It's not that I didn't still cry as I watched my angel daddy suffer through cancer, and it's not that I didn't wrestle with the fact that there was no more money in the bank account. It's that God began to show me the reality of finding His power and presence in the dark in spite of the problems that persisted.

Sometimes when life is dark, we lose our way and go off the deep end into obvious rebellion, relishing in things that are contrary to God and His Word. But when we learn to run to God in the dark and cling to Him when life seems dim, we discover the truth about victory in His presence. Victory doesn't mean we will be free from failure or future problems. It means we will be found in His presence when we feel lost and alone.

Learning to love God and live with Him daily is a decision we all must make. But God's decision was made a long time ago. When He sent Jesus to die for you and me and all humanity, He chose to give grace and mercy in the place of our sin. So all our running and rushing and ruining His plans is covered by the blood of Jesus.

When our problems make us question Him and call on Him, it's not a bad thing. It's a blessed thing. Anything that causes us to call on the name of Jesus is a blessing in disguise. It's a tangible gift of God's love for us.

When cancer interrupts life, we run to God.

When financial struggle sabotages us, we run to God.

When illness terrifies us, we run to God.

When abandonment wrecks us, we run to God.

These problems, these hard things we face in life, aren't meant to harm us; they are meant to heal us from the inside out.

Two days after Christmas, the entire family loaded in the van and went to the cancer center where my angel dad would have his final chemotherapy treatment. We sat all day as the minutes ticked away second by second. People came and went who were affected by the dreaded C word. Every race and age was represented. Cancer doesn't wait until a certain age or target a particular nationality. It attacks at random and doesn't always respond to the treatments. But sometimes it does. Sometimes the treatment kills the cancer, but we never know when cancer will return. Once it infects a body, it makes a person live on edge, on high alert of cancer's return.

In many treatment centers, there is a special bell that patients get to ring when their treatment is complete. We all stood with excitement and relief when it was Dad's turn to ring the bell. He walked down the hall with his changed physique, now thin and weak from the effects of the thing that is supposed to help him get better. He grabbed the rope that hung from the bell, and the sound of completion filled the doctors office full of people who hoped their turn would come too. We cheered and choked back surges of emotions that flooded the family. We walked out of the office relieved but educated. Although Dad's treatment was complete, we knew the cancer, the killer that so quietly crept in, might return at any moment. Close monitoring over the next several

Victory is surrender.

years would be necessary to catch it quickly and start a new series of treatments at its first sign of return.

The spiritual enemy imitates the silent killer, often creeping in and affecting the most unsuspecting victim. It waits for the opportunity to inflict pain and destruction, slowly growing until the disease is uncontrollable. Victory can only be experienced when treatment is consistent with close monitoring, which can take years. There is no bell ringing that completes the process. Cancer has given me a new dependence on God. I know that no matter how healthy we live or how much we focus on doing the right thing, cancer can still get into our family. The cancer of sin is looming at every turn just the same. Just as physical cancer has made me aware of my dependence on God and my surrender to His presence, spiritual cancer makes me aware of my need even more. It's just when I think I have it all together that everything falls apart. Life isn't about living powerfully so I can be more powerful; it's about living surrendered so I can see, in God's power, the temptation of sin coming my way. The only way to avoid the pressure of Satan is to surrender to the surety of God's power.

> Now the serpent was more subtle than any beast of the field which the LORD God had made. And he said unto the woman, Yea, hath God said, Ye shall not eat of every tree of the garden? (Genesis 3:1 KJV)

The enemy causes us to question the truth of God's words, when Jesus calls us to the opposite. He says our very life is based on God's words.

> But he answered, "It is written, 'Man shall not live by bread alone, but by every word that comes from the mouth of God.'" (Matthew 4:4)

The life we live, the power we hold, the passion we desire—everything in our lives that is life-giving—is from God. Living anchored in God's power involves living a life knowing we need the words of God to empower us through everything we face. If we never have a need for God, we will never live near Him. Our burdens, our problems, our difficult times push us to a place of surrender. Unless the cancer gets too deep, then we live distant, far away from the power of God. We run. We hide. We wrestle. We wait for God to rescue us, and when He doesn't, we feel like we might die. We want to ring the bell and be done with the painful parts of life, but the cancer of sin continues to convince us we can do it all by ourselves. Like a toddler determined to succeed, we live trapped in our own stubbornness. Until we surrender our problems of this world, we will never know the power of God.

When Dad rang the bell, we knew there might be more pain. But we also knew that the only way to live was fully trusting God's control. Dad had months where he literally could not eat food while undergoing treatment. As we gathered around the table and indulged in our favorite foods, Dad was fed liquid through a tube. He never showed anger and never cursed God for the cancer. He patiently walked through the suffering, continually speaking the name of Jesus through his pain. He lived as Jesus said men should: by the very words of God.

Choose God's power over every problem that comes your way! It's worth it.

Although I would never wish problems on anyone, I am learning that when every umbrella of my life collapses, God's power can finally fill me. It's painful and piercing, but when God's power comforts my trembling soul, I see it so clearly. I could never experience God until I knew how desperately I really needed Him.

I know many in the midst of trials would say, "I don't need God that bad." But when we hit rock bottom with nowhere to turn, we change our minds. There is no other option. There is no other way. Jesus is the only way. The power of His Spirit is the only thing that will propel us from the depths of despair to the divine deliverance of God.

How do we change our ways and stop asking God that

question: "Why?" I don't know if we ever will. When the next wave rolls in higher than the last, we will probably still rise up drenched in water and sand and screaming with all our might, but when the tide rolls back out and we go with it into the deep, we will find God's power there. Right there in the depths of everything dark that we go through, we now can listen and let Him define the dreams we never knew we wanted. Living in victory isn't about getting everything we ever wanted. It's about receiving the power we never knew we needed.

The next problem will come and we will probably cry, but I'm looking forward to the day when I learn to finally stop asking "Why?" Maybe that day will never come, or maybe that's the key to it all. Perhaps asking God the questions that no one wants to say out loud is the real answer to it all. After all, He does say, "You will seek me and find me, when you seek me with all your heart" (Jeremiah 29:13).

So, What Is Victory?

Victory is surrender.

It's surrendering your heart when your head says this doesn't make sense.

It's surrendering your soul when your common sense says this is absurd.

It's surrendering your life when your literal analogy says this does not add up.

It's surrendering your desires when your dream says this isn't the intended destiny.

It's surrendering your purpose when your planning says this is not the way it was supposed to turn out.

It's surrendering your intentions when your insides churn with the unknowns that lie ahead.

It's surrendering your motives when your memory says there are no more options.

It's surrendering your thoughts when your thinking says you'll never make it through this.

It's surrendering your grief when your gut says there is no getting out of this.

It's surrendering your fear when your faith feels like it's failing.

It's surrendering your wounds when weakness tells you you'll never win.

It's surrendering your power when your problems pile up, blinding you from God's presence.

Surrender is always about giving up something so that something else can win. If we never let go of the things that bind us, we will never experience the power God holds to set us free from bondage. Living a power-full life has little to do with what we do and everything to do with how much we are willing to give up.

Surrender saves us! It welcomes victory in and lets us experience God's peace, power, and presence. All of those other things—wounds, failures, and fears—bind. They cause lives to live in bondage for years and years. But God holds the power to set every life free! A power-full life is available even in the darkest valley or the most frightening memory of your life. It's up to us to choose power over our problems—not our own power, and not the world's power, but God's amazing power.

How Do We Experience God's Power?

1. We listen to God's voice and obey Him.

2. We let God define the dream, and we follow Him wherever He leads.

3. We choose victory when everything in our minds tells us to hold on to the thing that binds us. We release it. We heal. We stay in God's presence and let His power propel us beyond what we ever dreamed possible.

There were times in my life I thought I would never be free from crying in the dark of night over being abandoned. But I am free! I. AM. FREE!

With the power of the Holy Spirit, you have access to that same freedom, that same power, and that same God. It's up to you to live in victory. Choose God's power over every problem that comes your way! It's worth it.

And the next time you are caught in the torrential downpour of life, let your own umbrella give way to the rain. Lift your hands! Look up to the sky! And tell God you know why. May God be glorified in every raindrop.

Love and blessings,
Micah

Questions to Ponder

1. What is keeping you from living in victory?

2. What is one thing you need to release so that it can be replaced with God's power?

3. What is the hardest part about releasing the thing you mentioned above?

4. What will you do today to experience God's power? (Here's a hint: Listen. Let God be louder than your problems.)

Praying God's Power

Dear Heavenly Father,

For everything in my life that hasn't gone the way I think it should have, I thank You. More than anything in this world I want to live anchored in Your power and experience Your presence. Although life is not easy, and so many things don't go my way, I trust You. I choose to seek You. Knowing I will find You in the depths of everything I face, gives me power to praise You. Deliver me from the depths of my problems, and give me a renewed desire to live anchored in Your presence every single day. No matter what I face, help me know that You are with me and within me. Fill me with Your Spirit so the next time I lift my voice in anguish asking the question "why?" I will remember the answer is always to know Your power deeply and experience Your presence directly.

In Jesus' name, amen.

Experiencing God's Presence

I bless the LORD who gives me counsel;
    in the night also my heart instructs me.
I have set the LORD always before me;
    because he is at my right hand, I shall not be
      shaken.

Therefore my heart is glad, and my whole being
      rejoices;
    my flesh also dwells secure.
For you will not abandon my soul to Sheol,
    or let your holy one see corruption.

You make known to me the path of life;
    in your presence there is fullness of joy;
    at your right hand are pleasures forevermore.

—Psalm 16:7-11

Books Don't Just Happen

Sometimes God calls us to be vulnerable and to uncover tender places of our hearts so that others may see Him and understand more about Him. Writing this book exposes things I have often only thought or said to myself. In this vulnerable, weak place I have found the power of God and the meaning of what Paul meant when he said, "When I am weak, then I am strong."

As I walked this unknown path of writing a book and launching it out into the world, there was an army of people who prayed for, loved, and supported me along the way. And without their support I might be rocking back and forth in the corner of a padded room.

First, and above all, Jesus, my all in all: You silence my fears and hold me when I tremble. Your glory! Not mine! You give me eyes to see and ears to hear. You help me understand and know the truth. "Thank you" seems so insufficient for the King of kings. All praise to God the Father for every word penned and read.

Rob, my biggest encourager: thank you for being kind when I wanted to read paragraphs and chapters aloud to you, or when I spouted off ideas that made no sense at all. Thank you for loving me at my worst and supporting me when I felt like giving up. The way you walk through struggles inspires me and proves God's strength to me. You are a priceless gift. Hannah, Madalyn, and Jaxon, thank you for being my biggest fans. I could not have written this book without your love and prayers. I pray you always care enough about others to share your story with them. Always remember that Jesus loves you and so do I! You know why mommy wrote the book. It's because I love ya!

Mom: my first editor and my prayer warrior. You are a gift! This book is a result of the amazing mom and nana that you are. Your faithful example kept me anchored when I didn't know which way was up. And Dad, your words of wisdom impact me. Your words of encouragement strengthen me. Jacob, your life is a testimony of God's power. Thank you for living this message.

Mom and Dad Maddox, your constant love and support is incomparable. You are the most generous people I know.

My heart sisters: Summer, Kelly, Trisha, Sara, Sarah, Denise, Christie, Lisa, Leigha, and Sabrina, your prayer support and love is etched in between every word. Thank you for loving me and for being my sister friends.

Drew and Judy, your example compels me to look to God in every season no matter how hard. You are a living testimony of God's power.

Elaine, Valerie, Michelle, Dee, Beth, Stevie, Becca, Missy, and Nila, the way you hold my arms up when I need it through fervent prayer brings me so much peace. Thank you for being prayer warriors in my corner!

Blythe, the first time we talked I knew God's hand was all over your life. Praise Him for the way this book came together. Thank you for being sensitive to God's direction and for helping me form and develop this message.

Dawn, Susan, Brenda, and all those behind the scenes at Abingdon Press, you are a true delight to work with. Thank you for sharing the desire to offer hope to a hurting world.

And to you, the one who picked up this book in hopes of finding relief, help, hope, and encouragement, my deepest desire is that you see Jesus and experience His Power. I love you, but so much more than that, Jesus does. Look to Him!

So let's join hands, lift them high, and say glory to God in the highest! Praise Jesus! And Hallelujah!

Now excuse me while I go dance in the kitchen with my Father.

Notes

Chapter 3: Power in the Dark

1. Scotty Smith, *Objects of His Affection: Coming Alive to the Compelling Love of God* (West Monroe, LA: Howard, 2001), 146.

Chapter 5: Power in My Mind

1. "How Many Thoughts Do We Have per Minute?" Reference .com, www.reference.com/world-view/many-thoughts-per-minute-cb 7fcf22ebbf8466#.

Chapter 6: Power in My Heart

1. Holley Gerth, *You're Going to Be Okay* (Grand Rapids: Revell, 2014), 138.

Chapter 8: Power in Position

1. Kara Tippets, *The Hardest Peace* (Colorado Springs: David C. Cook, 2014), 17.
2. Priscilla Shirer, *Discerning the Voice of God* (Chicago: Moody, 2012), 23.

Chapter 9: Power in Perspective

1. Francis Chan, *Crazy Love* (Colorado Springs: David C. Cook, 2008), 41.

Chapter 10: Step 1: Listen to His Voice

1. Pricilla Shirer, *Discerning the Voice of God* (Chicago: Moody, 2012), 68.
2. Francis Chan, *Crazy Love* (Colorado Springs: David C. Cook, 2008), 25.